ACTING PROFESSIONALLY
RAW FACTS ABOUT CAREERS IN ACTING

Fourth Edition

ROBERT COHEN
UNIVERSITY OF CALIFORNIA, IRVINE

Mayfield Publishing Company
Mountain View, California

Library of Congress Cataloging-in-Publication Data
Cohen, Robert, 1938-
    Acting professionally : raw facts about careers in acting / Robert
    Cohen. — 4th ed.
      p.   cm.
    Bibliography: p.
    ISBN 0-87484-940-3
    1. Acting—Vocational guidance—United States. I. Title.
PN2055.C57 1990
792'.028'02373—dc20   89-9284
                                            CIP

Manufactured in the United States of America
10 9 8 7 6

Mayfield Publishing Company
1240 Villa Street
Mountain View, California 94041

Sponsoring editor, Janet M. Beatty; production editor, Jean Mailander; manuscript
editor, Carol Dondrea; text and cover designer, Jeanne M. Schreiber. The text was
set in 10/12 Palatino and printed by Thomson-Shore, Inc.

PREFACE

Almost ten years have passed since the third edition went to press, so I have taken the occasion of a fourth edition to rewrite the entire book, page by page. Naturally, this has meant updating all the facts, and reporting wholly new developments, such as Eligible Performer status, and new trends, such as the increasing importance of casting directors on both coasts and the growth of regional unified auditions.

The fundamental reality of the actor's career, however, remains unchanged. It is a thrilling struggle at best, a tedious labor at worst, and a daunting undertaking in any event. Again, I had better quote William Shallert, now a past president of the Screen Actors Guild: "Making a living as an actor is like trying to cross a rapidly rushing river stepping from one slowly sinking rock to another slowly sinking rock."[1] It's my goal in this book to show you (as best I can) where the rocks are, and which ones might hold your weight.

ACKNOWLEDGMENTS

One of my many pleasures from teaching acting for twenty-five years is the continuing rapport I enjoy with many former students, a large number of whom now populate the theatre professions: as actors, agents, directors, producers, artistic directors, casting directors, TV-commercial performers, union executives, and stage photographers. To many of them I have turned, during the preparation of the four editions of this book, for counsel on sundry matters, and their assistance has been invaluable—as well as personally gratifying. Larry Lott, Jeff Greenberg, and Bruce Bouchard, contributors in many ways to earlier editions, were virtual collaborators in this one, going over every page with careful and wonderfully helpful attention and providing me counsel on hundreds of details. I am also grateful in the extreme to such theatre pros as Libby Appel, Robert Barton, Dudley Knight, Keith Fowler, Eli Simon, Mary Ellen White, Al Hamacher, John Shepard, Anne Bloom, Asaad Kelada, Barry Kraft, Jonathan Lovitz, Mary Ann McGarry, Ray Reinhardt, Lee Shallat, Patrick Stewart, Briana Burke, and Brian Thompson for their invaluable suggestions, assistance, and/or comments, which have helped to shape this current version.

To these, and to my many advisors in the previous editions, I am deeply indebted and warmly grateful.

CONTENTS

CHAPTER 1   THE WAY IT IS   1

  The Acting Industry   5
  The Gross   6
  Acting Finances   8
  The Art of the Acting Profession   12
  Developing a Mature Viewpoint   14
  Here's to You   15

CHAPTER 2   WHAT YOU WILL NEED   16

  Talent   17
  Personality   20
  "Looks" and "Type"   24
  Training and Experience   31
        University Training   32
        Commercial Training   37
        Apprenticeships   39
        A Word of Caution   40
  Contacts   40
  Commitment and Will to Succeed   44
  Attitude, Discipline, and Capacity for Psychological
      Adjustment   46
  Freedom from Entanglements and Inhibitions   50
  Good Information and Advice   52

The Trade Journals   52
Other Sources of Information   53
Luck   54

CHAPTER 3   THE FIRST DECISIONS   55
Your Goal   55
Your Starting Medium   56
Choosing a Home Base   58
Regional Theatre: The LORT–Stock–Dinner Circuit   58
Getting into Regional Theatres   64
Auditioning Locally   64
Auditioning in New York   67
Regional Combined Auditions   67
Regional Concentrations   70
The Big Towns   70
How to Choose?   71

CHAPTER 4   ESTABLISHING YOURSELF   74
A Dependable Source of Income   75
A Telephone and Telephone Answering Service   75
Photographs   76
Taking Your Own Photos   83
Film on Yourself   84
Resumes   84
Unions   93
Eligible Performers   97
Should You Join the Union?   98
Agents and Agencies   100
Finding and Getting an Agent   105
Interviewing an Agent   109
Managers   111
Rounds: Seeing the CDs   112
CD Workshops, Classes, and Seminars   114
Getting Known: Advertisements for Yourself   115

CHAPTER 5   ON THE MOVE: INTERVIEWS, AUDITIONS, AND GETTING THE JOB   117

Interviews   117
Auditions   121
Cold Readings   130
The Screen Test   133
Nondramatic Options   134
    Commercials   134
    Business Theatre: Industrial Shows   136
    Working as an "Extra"   137
The Job Offer   138
How Much Will You Make?   140
    Stage Roles   140
    Film/TV   143
    Moving Up   144

CHAPTER 6   OTHER OPPORTUNITIES   147

Outside the Industry   147
Comedy   149
Academic Theatre   150
Your Own Company   152
Other Theatre Jobs   154

APPENDIX   156

Where to Go for Published Information   157
Trade Papers   158
Listings Books   158
    New York and Hollywood Listings   159
Listings of Summer Theatres, Regional Theatres, Dinner Theatres, and Outdoor Theatres   160
Books Where YOU List   161
Books About Acting and Actors   162
Union Offices   164
Schools of Theatre and Acting   164
Where to Live in New York or Los Angeles   166
Notes   167

CHAPTER 1

THE WAY IT IS

Acting is fun.

It is one of the most sublime activities of the human species; one of the most thrilling things to do with one's time since human civilization began. Imagine playing Hamlet, Juliet, Hedda, or Luke Skywalker—to the amazement and envy of your friends. Imagine going on the Johnny Carson show, and wittily putting down your enemies. Imagine a lifetime spent with Shakespeare, Shaw, and the latter-day celebrities of stage, screen, and TV-land. My guess is, if you've picked up this book, then you've already imagined these scenes.

Yes, acting can plunk you squarely in the world of great art, magnificent literature, and rich and celebrated people. Acting is socially exciting, politically stimulating, and there are wonderful parties afterward.

Acting's a dream, right?

Right. But it's certainly not a way to make a living.

Not a *career* living, anyway, which is to say: not a reasonable salary, year after year; not a salary that will be sufficient for you to have a home, a family, and enough in your bank account to be able to take your parents out to eat once a month.

Of course, some people get to do this. Some people win lotteries, too. But you must begin this book by acknowledging one absolutely significant reality: The number of professional actors who make a living salary, *year after year*, is unbelievably small.

In a country with 150,000 professional sheet metal workers, 350,000 plumbers, 650,000 carpenters, and one million electricians, there are barely 3,000 career-level working professional actors—in all media combined. I'm speaking of working actors who get paid for it—year in and year out—over a minimum of, say, two or three decades.

Three thousand persons barely even constitutes a profession—one might in fact think of it as a club. Yet it's a club that everyone seems desperate to join. "Everybody wants to get into the act!" lamented the late Jimmy Durante. And that act is acting.

Why do people want to get into a club that barely supports its minuscule membership? Because acting is fun, as I said. Fun and apparently rewarding—when you make it. But there are other reasons, perhaps even more compelling, that make Americans in every state and county want to get into the act, however they can.

Look around you. Actors, the world believes, are very rich and very famous. Not even very famous—*super*famous. And rich and famous happen to be our two most appealing lifestyles—so television shows us—particularly among young people.

Actors are the prime topics of the supermarket-counter press. They utterly dominate *People* and *Us* magazines; outnumbering physicists, teachers, plumbers, bank presidents, gardeners, accountants, lighting technicians, high school principals, and neurosurgeons all put together.

The theatre's backstage has moved onstage: Actors celebrate their own precious existence on the public airwaves every day, often on nationwide TV shows dedicated to that purpose alone: *Entertainment Tonight* and *Showbiz Today*. Actors are featured weekly in the giant magazine-style entertainment sections of Sunday newspapers. Books of interviews with actors now come out two or three times a year; actors are the guests on *The Tonight Show* and *David Letterman* Monday through Friday; we are more apt to see actors in TV interviews than on stage or in the movies. And the biggest names in the acting business appear on the cover of *Time*, just like world leaders. And in the booming mini-epics of *Lifestyles of the Rich and Famous*, which just about says it all.

And some actors are certainly rich. Sylvester Stallone received $25 million to play in *Rocky IV*; that's one hundred and twenty-five times the salary of the president of the United States. Bill Cosby earned $100 million in 1987. He *gave* $20 million to his favorite college. Need we say more?

Well, there *is* more: celebrity yacht parties off the isle of Capri; garages filled with luxury automobiles; penthouses atop various Trump Towers on a variety of coasts; triumphant stage and concert tours to London, Bangkok, and Tokyo; exotic location shooting in tropical paradises; stimulating friendships and glamorous love affairs; and, of course, dozens of people always around to carry the bags, cater the meals, and supply the continual adoration and companionship.

Yesterday's star has become today's superstar, bursting the very confines of heaven itself. The superstar is now the superartist, the superintellectual. No longer merely a rich celebrity, but spokesperson for the poor, savior of the animals, teacher of the unfit, mayor of Carmel and Palm Springs, consort of European royalty, and, until recently, president of the United States. Superstars are no longer merely heroes to the profession; they have become role models to the public, assuming the capabilities (additional to their own) of the characters they play. Jane Fonda and Jack Lemmon toured the United States, lecturing us on nuclear power. Why? Because they had acted roles in *The China Syndrome*, which was tangentially concerned with that subject. Jack Klugman testified to the U.S. Congress on the intricate matter of death certification policy—solely because he had once *performed* the TV role of a coroner. When the California insurance industry lost a $60 million constitutional initiative campaign, they decided to hire "a well-known actor . . . the industry's Cliff Robertson or Dennis Weaver . . . whose image will communicate integrity," to "interpret or testify in behalf of the industry on key questions and issues."[2] An actor's image, rather than a leader's deeds, is called upon to "communicate integrity" in today's world.

When the U.S. Senate Agriculture Committee investigated farm foreclosures, it called as chief witnesses such experts as Jane Fonda, Sissy Spacek, and Jessica Lange—because, naturally, these actresses had *played* farmwomen in movies about foreclosures. And Mmes. Fonda, Spacek, and Lange got—need we guess?—a *standing ovation* from the awed and august senators.

And, of course, Jane Fonda has now moved beyond her farmwoman (and nuclear power, and Vietnam War) expertise to become our national physical conditioning authority, competing with other such experts in nutrition and kinesiotherapy as Raquel Welch and the ubiquitous Cher.

All well and good, but it leads to a problem: namely, that to a young high school or college student, a career in acting seems to offer—in addition to respectability and a living wage—the real potential of world-dominating power and moral authority, together with intellectual attention, bohemian freedom, artistic admiration, international fame, and extraordinary wealth.

Moreover, such a career seems to require, by way of entry, no knowledge of languages, no study of mathematics or hard sciences, no laborious training, and no previous record of identified talent—such as violin virtuosity, skill at throwing the split finger curve, or even a C+ average.

Naturally, therefore, almost every forward looking young student, at some time or other, dreams about becoming an actor. Perhaps, as it happens, you dream about this too.

The problem is that for all but a tiny fraction of such dreamers, the dream is all but unattainable.

Acting is one of the toughest businesses to crack, perhaps it's *the* toughest.

It is certainly the most formidable of the organized professional arts, and almost all who seek to enter the profession—and live a reasonable part of their lives there—will fail to do so.

There is a staggering oversupply of actors, a virtual glut of both veteran professionals and inexperienced hopefuls—and the competition for work is unbelievably fierce, and getting fiercer.

At any one time, 85% of the members of the Screen Actors Guild (the film and television acting union) are *out of work*. And even more— 88%—of Actors' Equity Association (stage) actors are unemployed, too.

So, I do not intend, in this book, to be overly optimistic (I might say "falsely optimistic") about your, or anybody else's, chances. If I discourage some people, I will have saved them a lot of time and trouble— and reduced a bit of the actor glut for everybody else.

Having said that, I wish to make clear that I have no intention of being grim. Acting *is* fun, it is joyous, it is intensely rewarding, it is a terrific way to spend your life (or part of your life), and, yes, the professional rewards *are* there for those few who manage to overcome the extraordinary rigors of passage. And some do manage it. You already know who many of them are.

Acting also demands a tremendous amount of work, of *hard* work— and hard work is absolutely thrilling when it's directed toward a good and useful purpose. The theatre *is* a good and useful purpose; it is worth dedicating your life to, or at least a good part of your life—if you really know what you're doing and where you're headed.

It is my view that hard work can only be performed when you have a realistic notion of where the ground leaves off and the sky begins. That's what I am going to talk about in the pages that follow. The premise of this book is that it is better to know what difficulties lie ahead, so you can plan how hard you're going to have to work, than to laze about in a fantasy, waiting to be discovered while sipping sodas at a Hollywood lunch counter or waiting on tables at a Broadway delicatessen.

In what follows, therefore, I aim to set some level ground underfoot, and to provide the facts and guidance that might help any aspiring actor to make informed and effective career decisions.

Let's do it.

THE ACTING INDUSTRY

Whatever else acting might be, it is a *job*, and a job within one of America's biggest enterprises: the entertainment industry. You should be aware of the scale of the actor's larger world.

The Broadway theatre generates, for its owners, an income of more than a quarter-billion dollars a year, and the national road companies of Broadway shows generate a like amount. That's about $500 million in revenues each year. When you add in the regional, summer, and dinner theatres, you've got a billion-dollar industry in live theatre alone.

A Broadway play costs $1 to $2 million to mount, and a Broadway musical can run about $6 to $8 million. Any show can lose that whole amount on opening night; several have.

But theatre revenues are piddling compared to television and films. Television, which provides by far the greatest income for America's professional actors, is dominated by three networks, each of which, even in decline, earns and spends more than $2 billion a year. The film industry, which is now interlocked with resort hotels, book publishing, amusement parks, recording studios, soft drink bottling plants, pinball machines, and gambling casinos, recorded a record box office take in 1988 of close to $4.4 billion. The film *E.T. alone* has taken in over a quarter-billion dollars in rental fees, and virtually a like amount in videocassette sales. It will soon have the gross national product of a small Third World nation. So does the "Bill Cosby Show," of which syndicated reruns alone have brought its producers half a billion dollars.

These sums are enormous, even in America's inflated business climate. Overall, the entertainment industry provides the second largest United States' export product (after airplanes), bringing in about $5 billion a year from abroad—in times when the United States is a debtor nation in virtually all other respects. And it's *growing*; the American professional entertainment industry is increasing revenues twice as fast as is the professional spectator sports industry. Acting may be an art, but it is also part of (if not buried in) a giant capital enterprise: the American socioeconomic system. And you must find a role in that system.

As with any industry, behemoth bureaucracies are well implanted. The seven major film studios are now all subsidiaries of huge international conglomerates. Thus, the company that makes Paramount Pictures (formerly Gulf and Western, now Paramount Communications) also owns sports arenas and publishing companies. Similarly, Columbia Pictures is owned by Coca-Cola; United Artists is owned by Australia's Qintex Group, 20th Century Fox is part of Australia's News Corporation, and Universal Studios is a subsidiary operation of the giant Music Corporation of America (MCA)—which itself is reportedly being wooed by Japan's Sony Corporation as well as Nippon Steel. "The film business," reports one observer, "in the end looks more like a conglomerateur's hobby."[3] So, for that matter, does TV: NBC is a subsidiary of General Electric, and both CBS and ABC are part of much larger music and book publishing systems. MTM Television, once the personal creation of actress Mary Tyler Moore, is now an international megaproduction company owned by Television South P.L.C. in Great Britain. The commercial legitimate theatre, for its part, is dominated by like oligopolies. Just three families (the Shuberts, the Nederlanders, and the Jujamycns) own virtually all of New York's Broadway theatres, as well as most of the commercial touring playhouses in the United States. And the financing for their operations—when they don't generate it themselves—often comes from the film and television conglomerates.

That acting is part of America's big business is a fact with which every actor must reckon. "Actors must understand this is a business and treat it as a business," says Hollywood casting director Francine Witkin. "They're a *product*. Most people don't think of themselves as products, they think of themselves as human beings with fantasies and dreams. They've got to realize what this business is and what the politics are."[4]

THE GROSS

What the business and politics come down to, of course, is money. Money in that quaint but apt show business term, the "gross," which is short for "gross receipts." "Amazing Grace Grosses!" screams a headline in *Variety*, explaining that the film *Amazing Grace* has had an "amazing gross" of so many dollars in its opening week. More than a few young actors have wondered if they hadn't picked up the wrong newspaper when they took their first look at *Variety*, the show business weekly (and in Hollywood a daily) that is the bible of the industry. "Grosses" are the prime news on every page, and the prime concern of every "suit" in the business.

"Suit": *n.*, what Hollywood actors call studio office personnel; in general, anyone who wears a business suit, other than as a costume.

The gross is always the bottom line, and, yes, a certain grossness in the moral sense also pervades the business end of the acting industries, particularly in Hollywood. Lying, stealing, and lawsuits—well-known features of the film trade—are described with candor and wit by William Bayer in his excellent and still very pertinent *Breaking Through, Selling Out, Dropping Dead* (see the bibliography). An even more contemporary picture of gross Hollywood politics, fiscal and sexual, is given in famed playwright/film director David Mamet's 1988 play, *Speed the Plow*.

And, yes, just as you've heard, sexual politics is very much a part of the grossness, too. In *Final Cut*, writer/director Paul Sylbert details his experiences in making the film *The Steagle* and tells how he was pressured to cast the mistress of an Avco Corporation executive (Avco then owned Embassy Pictures) in a featured part.[5]

And while Hollywood may be more fun to talk about, Broadway is just as conscious of the bottom line. In Mamet's *Speed the Plow* (produced by a nonprofit theatre), the leading actress (Madonna) was certainly not cast as much for her thespian skills, though considerable, as for the gross receipts that a rock star might (and did) attract. Neither moralist Mamet nor nonprofit Lincoln Center shied from the bottom line here.

Even the purest are not invulnerable to the grossest appeals. A highly publicized invitation for the late John Wayne to receive a "worst actor" award from the Harvard *Lampoon* was actually a publicity stunt worked out between the Warner Brothers' Studio and Harvard. "One of the biggest media breaks for a film biz publicity stunt in recent memory of trade toutmasters," beamed the *Variety* reporter of this concocted puffery between Harvard ("No, not Harvard!"), John Wayne ("Say it ain't so, Duke!!"), and the ever-present Hollywood "toutmasters."

So where do actors fit into the gross? I'm afraid right at the bottom. In the legitimate theatre, actors receive only about 10% of the overall cash flow (about $125 million of a $1+ billion business in 1988). In film, the actors earn even less—only about 4% of what crosses the producer's desks ($187 million out of $4.38 *billion*—in domestic rentals only—in 1988). And in TV, actors earn an even smaller share of the overall income ultimately flowing to the fiscal movers and shakers: the network corporations, the station owners, and the programmers and producers.

Although by far the most visible workers in both dramatic and cinematic industries, and the most known (and worshipped) by the theatregoing and filmgoing public, professional actors therefore account for but a tiny share of the power and profits.

But are actors valued in other ways? Oh, the Tonys and Oscars are nice for the ego, but the real power lies elsewhere. In *The Movie Business: American Film Industry Practice*, only 1 chapter out of 34 (representing 4 pages of 370) deals with actors (the chapter is entitled "Actors as Union Men"). And the section called "Creative Functions" has five chapters: "The Producer," "The Director," "The Team Producer," "The Writer/Producer," and "The Low Budget Producer"—the actor is not even deemed a contributor to the creative function![6] In theatre companies, the term "artistic staff" generally refers to the director, the designers, and sometimes the producers—never the actors. Clearly, actors are not the celebrities in their industries that they are in the fan magazines.

So, what is life like in and around these industries? Bruce Bouchard, now a co-artistic director of Capital Repertory Company in Albany, wrote from New York three years after he arrived in town: "It's impossible. It's for mad people. I mean absolutely insane lunatics have to want to go into this business. There's no security for anyone. And in a business when the work is the only reality you've got, and there's no work, it can beat the hell out of you." And this was from a young man who got cast the week he got to town, and whose career since then could easily be portrayed, at least from the outside, as an unbroken stream of successes. The moral: NO acting career is an unbroken stream of anything—least of all successes.

ACTING FINANCES

Young people often have one of two financial goals in mind when they begin to think of acting professionally. The first is their "adolescent" goal: They want to be movie stars and make piles and piles of money.

But they soon put that aside for a second, more considered, "mature," and "realistic" goal: Now they scorn the piles of money, and seek only a steady acting job—probably with a modest repertory company in a medium-sized town—with security and artistic respectability. Rejecting riches, they opt for a reasonable salary—"just enough to live on."

Well enough, but the problem is simply that the so-called "mature" goal is just about as hard (maybe even harder) to achieve as the so-called "adolescent" one!

Big surprise: Merely rejecting Broadway and Hollywood does not magically produce something else in its place, any more than rejecting an unoffered BMW will put a Hyundai in your driveway.

The fact is that the supply of actors so overwhelmingly exceeds the demand that you will have to be one in a hundred to get *any* paid acting job. One in a hundred, *literally*—and maybe even one in a thousand.

New York and L.A. veterans often blithely give this advice to a young actor: "Why, just get a small part in a regional theatre, and you can go from there." *Just* get a small part? The advice is sound, but the tone isn't if it implies that it is easier to get a professional role in Indiana than in Los Angeles. In fact, it may be harder to get that job in Indiana. The fundamental fact is that employment in *any* of the acting industries is simply very, very, very difficult to get; and an actor with superb college drama credentials should no more simply expect to get a paid acting job than a first-rate political science graduate should expect to become a United States senator. Hope, yes; expect, no.

And don't think that you can negotiate for a starting professional job by offering to take it at a low price: That's all it's going to pay anyway. And *everybody's* price is low in this business. Why is that? Because most of your competitors are just as hungry for work as you are (they, too, read *People* magazine and watch *Entertainment Tonight*). For producers, it's a buyer's market, and union-negotiated minimum wages are often maximum wages as well. In any event, because so many actors are willing to work at minimum, your economic bargaining power as a beginner is nonexistent, and any offer to work at scab rates, should you be foolish enough to make one, will be rejected out of hand.

Then you should learn another lesson: There's not that much money in acting anyway. How much income do actors really make? Not what you might expect from the magazines at the supermarket check-out stand.

There are about 37,000 active, paid-up members of Actors' Equity Association, but only a little more than a third of them (13,641) managed to get any work at all during 1988. Only 2,231 of them—about 6% of the total number of unionized professional stage actors in this country—earned as much as $15,000 that year. And $15,000 a year is ordinarily less than the starting pay for a secretary anywhere else, but 94% of America's professional stage actors made less than that acting on stage in 1988.

The median income for working Equity actors (i.e., for those 37% of the actors who actually worked) was only $4,371 for 1988. Can they live on that? The government poverty line for a single person that year was about $5,720; that's more than $1,300 higher than the median actor's salary. So the average working Equity actor earned about $112 per month *under* the official U.S. per-person poverty level, and fully half the working actors made even less than that. And that's *working* actors. The median income for *all* Equity actors was simply nothing (right, that's $0.00 for the year), since almost two-thirds of them were totally unemployed for all of 1988. And, most likely, for 1987 as well, as a matter of fact.

Of course, there's more money in film and TV, and stage actors usually try to supplement their income there ("Theatre is the most artistically fulfilling, but film and TV are still where actors make a living," says Equity executive Guy Pace). But that's often easier said than done, too. In truth, film and television actors fare only marginally better, and then mainly because of commercials. There are 69,000 members of the Screen Actors Guild, but rarely are more than 10% working at any one time. In 1986, 30% of the SAG membership had no income whatever, and another third of them worked only five days or less for the whole year.

Worse news yet: A recent study by the Labor Institute for Human Enrichment found that actors don't even get their fair share of unemployment benefits; in fact, less than half do. Why? "Infrequent job continuity and long periods of unemployment . . . prevent performers from compiling sufficient work experience to meet the qualifications for benefits," LIFHE found out.

Let's face it; we're talking real poverty here. Nor, given the continuing glut of actors and would-be actors, is there much impetus to improve things. The Actors' Equity Association is probably the only union in the history of trade unionism to negotiate a contract *downward*—to where its members could work for *free* (the late Equity waiver plan), and, while a laughable $5 minimum performance fee (that's not a misprint) is currently in place in the Los Angeles theatre, one wonders if the actor will not always be at the bottom of the barrel. Indeed, the $5 minimum fee is often halved, with Equity's consent, to $2.50 a day (that's right: two dollars and fifty *cents*), if the producer can demonstrate sufficient fiscal angst. The situation for actors is not getting better, it's getting worse.

While the total number of work weeks for stage actors has increased slightly since 1968 (by 40%, or 2% per year), the actual income, measured in constant dollars, is down. (The work week increase has occurred wholly in the regional theatre, where salaries are relatively low, at the expense of the higher-paying Broadway and touring contracts, which have fallen substantially.) But the number of actors is up—*way* up! The total number of professional stage actor work weeks has increased by 40%, whereas Equity membership has increased by 160%. That means that since the first edition of this book, the *number of professional stage actors has grown four times faster than the number of jobs*. And the number of would-be professional actors has probably grown ten times faster.

It should be no surprise, then, that although 66% of Equity's members were employed during 1968, only 37% were employed in 1988. And while 24.7% worked any given week in 1968; only 11.9% did twenty years later.

Unemployment is, in other words, simply the prevailing (and increasing) reality of the actor's life. It is no wonder the basic policy for theatrical producers is to hire at "scale," for, according to a producer's handbook of advice, "Almost always the cast is hired for the Equity minimum, and their greater remuneration comes from the opportunity to work."[7] Such greater remuneration, however, does not pay the rent.

When work is even scarcer, actors *pay* to work. During the SAG actor's strike of 1988, hundreds of actors produced their own plays, at their own expense, just to keep their faces before the public. And most showcases in both New York and L.A. are paid for by the actors who participate in them.

TV and films aren't exactly a growth industry either. Nonacting programming (game shows, talk shows, documentaries, televangelists, shopping shows, and so-called "reality shows") have recently proliferated, and the new cable companies and superstations now making serious inroads on the networks often rely on repackaging old films, sitcoms, and cartoons. Cost-cutting applies as well throughout the declining networks. "We're talking some deaths, we're talking some disappearances, we're talking some escapes," said Jeff Frielich, executive producer of CBS's *Falcon Crest*, explaining that three prime-time serials had reduced the number of actors in an effort to reduce production costs. "With other costs going up," said Frielich, "the most logical place to make cuts is the cast."[8]

So one mustn't take the extravagance of *Lifestyles of the Rich and Famous* too much to heart, at least where actors are concerned. Few other than starring performers will accumulate anything resembling even the incomes (or lifestyles) of gardeners, plumbers, secretaries, or schoolteachers. With jobs and income at a minimum, actors have little chance to earn, less chance to save. And even when an actor finds work—when the ten-week run ends—he or she is back on the street, just as before, looking for work.

But they still come. For every union actor pounding the pavements of New York, or circling the freeways of Hollywood, there are a hundred shadow actors in the wings.

There are over fifteen hundred college and university drama departments today graduating students ambitious to act professionally. And there are another thousand or so conservatories, professional schools, private coaches, and theatre institutes, plus uncounted community theatres, high school teachers, and stage mothers—all pointing their charges in the same direction.

And there are also the legions of bored housewives, harried executives, ambitious models, starry-eyed television announcers, overage running backs and high divers, teenage shopgirls, ex-mayors and ex-presidents, surf bums, and ski bums who are right now pondering the possibilities of making it into Hollywoodland or the Great White Way. These people are in competition with every actor in the business. They are also *your* competition. Among them are thousands who are, let's face it, talented, hardworking, persistent, and dedicated, and who carry with them glowing reviews from the *Denver Post*, the *New Haven Register*, and the *Fresno Bee*. They all have the same idea you have—to develop a successful acting career—and some of them may even be more cutthroat and determined than you are!

THE ART OF THE ACTING PROFESSION

It is clear from the foregoing that most actors live at a standard well below the established poverty level—which creates enormous problems for people who not only have to live, eat, and stay healthy, but who must dress well, look well, buy photographs, and get to auditions. Still, most actors are willing to put up with financial deprivation, at least for a while, because they are pursuing something far more important than money. They are pursuing their "art." A few more worms may lurk in these strawberry fields, however.

A well-known film producer used to send a telegram to the cast of every new picture on the first day of shooting. The message was "Forget art, make money." ("Forget" was not the word he chose, but it was one that Western Union would send over their lines.) Most producers—although they're usually mum about it—live by this sentiment, and consequently a huge amount of purely commercial claptrap is marketed in Hollywood, in New York, and even in the resident regional theatres. Some producers actually brag about it. In the words of one midwestern theatrical producer/director: "I am not in the theatre business, darling. I am in the ass business. I am in the business of putting asses in my seats."

A review of the film *The Love Machine* in *Variety* made this cynical but significant point: "The secret of a film like this, rarely spoken outside of inner sanctums, is that if it were better written, better directed, and better acted, it would probably fail." The gross wins out, time and again.

You can't ever forget: The industry's primary goal is to make money, and your value to the industry is determined precisely (and often solely) by how much money you can make for it. Art and originality are at best secondary considerations in most industry enterprises, and no "new wave" or "new theatre" has been able to change this principle—not, at least, as it applies to you making your living as an actor.

Perhaps New York is a more artistic acting milieu than Hollywood, as is often supposed, and perhaps regional repertory, with its more varied demands and nonprofit atmosphere, provides a purer artistic climate yet (a less commercial climate, anyway) than either of America's two major metropolitan theatre centers. But I doubt it. There may be some truth to these generalizations, but generalizations they remain. There is great art and integrity where there are great artists and decent people, and they exist everywhere in the business, in Hollywood as much as anywhere else. But you'll find enough avarice, deception, and exploitation to fill several trash novels. You're going into the real world, and you're going to have to learn to be a skilled judge of character, and how to tread effectively between making art and making money.

DEVELOPING A MATURE VIEWPOINT

There are some hard lessons in the previous paragraphs, but they are basic adult realities, and they are lessons worth learning.

If you're going to pursue an acting career, you're going to have to deal with adult reality, and you're going to have to be an adult—while retaining enough of the childlike innocence required for any artist.

What does being an adult mean? It means, basically, that *you*—not your parents or teachers—will be taking the initiatives in your own life. You will be making (and responding to) your own assignments, as it were.

The biggest difference between life as a student and life after graduation is that, after graduation, nobody assigns you anything. Nobody tells you what to do next. Nobody *cares* what you do next. And there are no grades.

As wonderful as this may seem, it can lead to life's first great agonies: What do I do now? How good am I? Am I going to make it? Why doesn't anybody care about me?

Nobody in the adult world will answer those questions—unless you pay them to (in which case they are not unbiased) or unless they love you (in which case they are even more certainly not unbiased).

The rest of this book is to help you deal with these questions.

One thing to get out of your system right away, if you want to be an actor, is a desperate need for praise.

Praise is so easily given, and so inexpensive to part with, as to be functionally meaningless (and cruelly misleading) in the adult world, where it is mainly a soothing balm in the often abrasive world of doing business. It costs nothing (and therefore means nothing) for a casting director to say, "Oh, you're very talented, I love your audition!" So they say it all the time. It's simply the easiest (and safest) way to turn you down. "Hollywood is the only place where you can die of encouragement," says Pauline Kael.[9] Nothing is more depressing than to hear actors coming back from auditions exclaiming enthusiastically, "I didn't get the part, but I feel that they *liked* me!" It's depressing because actors don't audition to be liked, but to be hired. Acting professionally is a business: What difference does it make if they like you if they never hire you? And *do* they like you? Maybe they're just trying to get rid of you. Some actors hang around for years subsisting on such dollops of empty praise.

Praise is an incentive to children. It is the A+ or the gold star or the pat on the back that induces good study habits and good behavior.

But praise is mainly a lubricant in an adult business that generates enormous friction and despair among its participants. Praise is doled out by worldly-wise producers—mainly to keep you from coming back to bomb their house or kidnap their children. They may give you praise when you seem to need it, but they will give you a job only when *they* need it. And that's where you have to learn to fit in.

HERE'S TO YOU

If you've read this far, and haven't yet thrown the book against the wall, you might just have a chance.

If you suspect that discussions of the past few pages have been designed to alarm you, your suspicions are correct.

There are much pleasanter things to say about acting as a profession, and much more positive advice to be given. The rest of the book will be in this direction.

Still, at this point, it's essential to keep before us this fact: Acting is a profession that hasn't very much room for you, and isn't going to be welcoming you to its inner sanctums. The unions, in fact, will be very actively trying to keep you out. There is hardly a single producer, director, actor, or union executive who will not *routinely* advise aspiring actors not to press on. Don't put your daughter on the stage, Mrs. Worthington, Don't put your daughter on the stage. I have no hesitation in repeating Noel Coward's famous lyric, because the people who will press on are going to press on anyway. And they're probably among the few who are going to make it, too.

CHAPTER 2

WHAT YOU WILL NEED

If you are going to make it—that is, if you are going to make a livelihood as an actor—then you must possess the following:

- Talent
- A charming / fascinating / interesting / likable /hateful definable *personality*
- Looks, and certain physical characteristics
- Training
- Experience
- Contacts
- Commitment and a massive will to succeed
- A healthy attitude and a capacity for psychological adjustment
- Freedom from entanglements and inhibitions
- Good information, advice, and help
- Luck

You might want to rebel at some of these items, such as "contacts," "looks," or "freedom from inhibitions." But these requirements should not be understood in a negative sense. You do not have to be the son of a film editor, or a Miss Georgia contestant, to succeed as an actor— and you certainly do not have to sleep with the casting director. Developing contacts, becoming flexible in your acting, and caring for your personal health, however, are extremely important to career success.   Each of the requirements listed is a basic ingredient for professional work, and each deserves a full discussion.

TALENT

I'm afraid the first requirement for success still is acting talent. It is of far greater importance than any other factor. Talent is the *sine qua non* of a performer, and while there are certainly those who make a brief professional appearance without it, lasting success comes only to those who have it.

But what the hell *is* it? And do *you* have it?   Well, these are questions on which neuroses are based.

"Talent: I can't define it, but I know it when I see it." Almost everyone says this, one way or another, and it makes perfectly good sense. Talent is essentially a kind of *communication*. And since it is mostly nonverbal, it is not defined so much as it is recognized. "Magnetism," "electricity," stage "presence"—these are the metaphors we use to discuss talent, describing those qualities that make a person communicate (project) a compelling personality, without simply pushing themselves on us.

Talent is a *two-way exchange* with the audience. It's not simply something you have within you, but it's also your ability to interact with an audience. To share—give and take—with an audience. We, the audience, will define your talent as much as you, the actor, will reveal it.

Personal magnetism or "electricity" (think of it as "alternating current") is the ability to draw others to you, to inspire them, to lead them with your words, your body, and your eyes. It is the ability to establish rapport, and set up mutual vibrations, both intellectually and emotionally. It is the ability to enter into mutual feedback with other actors, and with an audience as well.

Confidence is central to talent; some say talent is *only* that. Confidence is the power you have over your own personality; it allows you to be unafraid in your own persona, to stand tall and easy on your own feet, to accept criticism freely—and at the same time to rise above it. *You* have to develop this confidence too, of course. Think of it as a test of your talent, rather than as a subservience to your critics.

Talent allows you to *believe* in yourself: in the reality of your performance, and in the reality of your "being an actor"—even when no one else does. You may have substantial doubts about your potential for long-term career success, but you can never doubt that you "are" an actor. That is a belief that must be in your bones, sustaining itself through every interview and every audition, so that it shows even though you make no *effort* to show it. This belief is your authority; it gives you the power that allows you to galvanize every aspect of personality and every bit of training and experience into an exciting and apparently artless performance or audition.

Do you have talent? How do you tell? You can't rely on mere compliments, good grades, or the old devil word: praise. Rather note this: As a performer, you should be *getting cast.* In college or in neighborhood plays, you should be auditioning for—*and getting*—major roles, or at least you should be regularly considered for them. If, after two or three years of training as an actor, you are still unsuccessful at getting major roles in college or community theatre productions, and if they're going to people you think are less than terrific, (and, of course, if your casting is not being hampered by political considerations beyond your control), you should begin to reconsider your career goals. Tough advice, but better now than later. "Major" roles, of course, are not defined just by size; they are the roles you *want* to play, the roles you think you *ought* to play. While it may be perfectly true that "there are no small roles, only small actors," the fact remains that only a major role will fully expand and test your abilities. The size of a role is not always of primary consequence; the depth, breadth, wit, passion, individuality, and "electricity" of the role are the characteristics that determine whether it provides this sort of talent test.

In general, the people who rise to successful careers and even stardom are recognized as very talented from the very beginning. Craft and experience can be acquired along the way, but talent, where it exists, shows up almost immediately.

On the other hand, extraordinary talent does not mean perfection of performance or anything close to it. Extraordinarily talented people have been known to sink in one disaster after another. They perform badly, they cannot be heard, they aren't believable, they do the same thing over and over, they get too fat or too thin, they're always committing some terrible error or other, and they frequently reap the derision of their peers, teachers, and even their directors. *But they always get cast.* Hardly anyone had a good thing to say about Stacy Keach or Daniel Travanti or Joan Van Ark when they were students at the Yale Drama School in the mid-1960s, for example. The other acting students gravely discussed their supposed acting problems, and the Yale teachers often despaired of their ability to master class assignments. But they took all the leading roles of the year, and directors fought like wildcats over them; they are now, of course, major stage and film/TV performers. Their talents were simply enormous and obvious, inciting ample peer jealousy—along with leading roles.

Talent means all that we have discussed, and more still. It *can* mean, in addition:

- That a person sings, dances, juggles, tells jokes, walks tight-ropes, or does striptease, backflips, handsprings, or T'ai Chi. Most talented people can do some of these; many more think they are talented because they can do one or two. A person who is genuinely talented need not be able to sing on key, but can probably "sell" a song if called upon to do so. The more skills a person has, obviously, the more employable he or she is.

- That a person can communicate nuances clearly yet subtly. That an actor can vary inflection and timing so as to communicate what a director wants, without excessive coaching or rework-ing. Whether the actor does this by technique or instinct is not the concern of this book, but that the actor must be *able* to do it, and do it rapidly, particularly during an audition, everyone agrees.

- That a person has a flexible, mobile, and expressive voice and body. These are the actor's basic tools. At the outset, the actor must be in possession of an expressive speaking voice:one that communicates what is between the lines , one that connotes something beyond the mere words spoken. Similarly, the tal ented person communicates in body movement and repose, naturally assumes interesting positions and postures, and is— yes—attractive to look at. Sex appeal is obviously related to this, and although that is not by a long shot the whole story, it is clear that an audience sensually intrigued is an audience already on its way to admiring and relishing a performance. Casting directors have never been oblivious to this, and you shouldn't be, either.

- That a person is relaxed in front of others, and when per-forming for others, and *enjoys* performing. This enjoyment is said to result from an exhibitionistic instinct, and nothing in our experience contradicts that. Though actors may be as shy as anyone else (and not a few of them are painfully shy), some part of their personality relishes contact with others, even via the formal medium of theatre or film.

These are all aspects of "talent," and the word is often used to denote one or more of them. There are no firm prerequisites for "making it" in show business, but the necessity for talent comes as close as any possibly could.

PERSONALITY

Personality is the second most important characteristic of the successful actor, a ranking that often draws shrieks of dismay. "What does my personality have to do with it? Use me for my talent and ability. My personality is my own business!" Sorry, but no. As the American actor William Gillette said more than three generations ago,

> Among those elements of Life and Vitality, but greatly surpassing all others in importance, is the human characteristic or essential quality which passes under the execrated name of Personality. The very word must send an unpleasant shudder through this highly sensitive Assembly; for it is supposed to be quite the proper and highly cultured thing to sneer at Personality as an altogether cheap affair and not worthy to be associated for a moment with what is highest in Dramatic Art. Nevertheless, cheap or otherwise, inartistic or otherwise, and whatever it really is or not, it is the most singularly important factor for infusing the Life-Illusion into modern stage creations that is known to man.[10]

Sixty years have not changed the import of Gillette's well-capitalized comments.

American film and theatre performances today remain dominated by the Stanislavski/Strasberg/*cinema verité* school of acting, in which the actor's innate qualities (read: personalities) reveal themselves in the characters they play. Whether one is happy or sad about this is immaterial. Even directors and producers who heap sarcasm and scorn on Stanislavski's "Method" generally cast their works, if unwittingly, according to basic Method precepts, seeking actors who can "live the life of their characters" on stage or before the camera. Actors who can live the life of their characters on stage are probably already living it when they walk in for their audition or interview.

Particularly in film and television, actors are cast largely on the basis of "personal quality." Major casting decisions, in the professional world, are largely made at the interview stage, long before auditions begin. And interviews are a test only of appearance and personality. For film and TV work, fifty or a hundred actors will usually be interviewed in order to find just four or five to audition; the four or five who are deemed to have the right "quality" for the role are then permitted to read for it. You can see, therefore, that in these cases fully 90% of the casting decision will be based on what you show *before* you have an opportunity to audition, and what you show is basically your person—and your personality. It's absolutely crucial. In the legitimate theatre, auditions weigh more heavily. However, even there, the importance of a stageworthy personality—one suited to the role, of course—is still enormously important.

The reasons for this are many. Directors are usually seeking believable naturalness, Mr. Gillette's "Life-Illusion," and they are under a lot of pressure to get it quickly—right away, if possible. Unlike Stanislavski, who had the luxury of nine to twelve month rehearsal periods, the modern American stage director must get good characterizations in a matter of three or four weeks; the film and television director often only a couple of days, and frequently only ten or fifteen *minutes.* In films, reports *M. Butterfly* star John Lithgow, "more often than not, you arrive, and you're expected to start acting immediately. The director hardly has a word to say to you. You'd be amazed. You arrive, the camera rolls, and you start acting. It's as simple as that."[11] As a normal television "day player," in a guest episodic role, you will be expected to appear on the set, maybe twenty-four hours after getting your script, lines learned and ready to shoot, at eight o'clock in the morning. After introductions and a quick rehearsal to hit the marks (blocking), the cameras roll; minutes later your scene is history, and the cast and crew are on to the next scene. Clearly in these cases there is simply *no time* to work at developing your character. Television directors, therefore, *must* use personality as a basis for casting.

The foundation of this short-order work is basically Stanislavski's "Magic If." What would you do "if" you are Linda, the delivery girl, in "L.A. Law" and Richard Dysart is yelling at you while your boyfriend is trying to get your attention? Linda will do it as *you* would do it, and Linda comes out looking a lot like you, which is why they cast you in the first place; that's how they saw Linda.

Acting in films is almost as rushed. Henry Fonda reports that of his ninety films, only five had the luxury of a rehearsal period in which characterization could be carefully developed. And while the legitimate theatre remains a medium where characterization can be created through the rehearsal process, that rehearsal process may be a lot shorter than yours was in college; and time—which is expensive in the professional world—is much more at a premium.   American stage directors, often working somewhat improvisationally, may seek to employ your personal characteristics and idiosyncrasies as much as possible, gaining thereby an individuality in your part otherwise unavailable. All this demands that a great portion of "the real you"— your own personality—be employed in the service of the performance.

Yet it is not sufficient merely to have a personality that is "right for the role." You must also have, or seem to have, a widely *appealing* or *exciting* personality. "Likability" is the crucial factor in acting, says professional actor manager Bud Robinson, and audience appeal (and audience excitement) translate readily into the fiscal bottom line.[12] In Hollywood, a numerical personality rating system, known as TVQ, is often used in casting decisions, and actors are awarded "Q scores" on the basis of what audiences think of them, *as people*. (Hollywood press agents hotly deny there is such a thing, and a *Los Angeles Times* article[13] called it "The Thing that doesn't exist." But it does exist. It's 1,400 pages long, costs $38,000, and reflects the "scientifically selected sample of 1,200 households" according to the *Times*.) Politically active performers, such as Jane Fonda and Ed Asner (who calls TVQ "McCarthyism"), have been hurt in the Q ratings, despite their unquestioned acting skills; less controversial actors have scored higher.   "A low Q score could spell disaster," says the Screen Actors Guild, in lamenting the TVQ's attempt to put a dollar value on an actor's perceived personality.

What is a good acting personality? It is no one thing in particular, but it is definable in general terms. You are shy, you are fascinating, you are profound, you are dangerous, you are aggressive, you are hostile, you are nasty, you are fiery, you are sensual, you are youthful, you are idealistic, you are wacky, you are serene.

A warning: That you are *nice* will get you nowhere. Nice isn't a personality. Thousands of aspiring actors have failed in interviews simply by being nice, polite, and forgotten. What's wrong with nice? It's proper enough, but it's also dull, it's unexciting, and it doesn't bring people into the theatres. Yes, I'm afraid, there *is* an "interview technique," and you will have to learn it (some tips are given in the following section). A hundred actors will grouse, "I didn't get the job because I don't play their games at the interview. I'm just not that kind of person." But it's not a game, and you *must become* that kind of person. Interview technique is nothing but letting other people see just what kind of person you are—*when you're not in an interview*. The trick is that you have to show this *in* an interview. This may in fact be the truest test of your acting! If your day-to-day personality is hidden in your interview behind a dozen "pleased-to-meet-yous" and a score of "thank-you-very-muches," you will never be looked at further. When you retreat into timid subservience at an interview, you not only fail to "play the interview game," you insist on playing another game: the "good little girl" or "good little boy" game that got you so far in the principal's office. Well, perhaps for the first time in your life, this is the wrong game to play.

Successful actors are not bland people. That is not to say that they are wantonly brash or abrasive. Most actors of my acquaintance are people with depth, sensitivity, dedication, and artistry. Their personalities are not applied for the sake of calling attention to themselves. The surest way to lose your personality is to spin out a fake one. Your real personality will follow you in every role you play; it will become your trademark. In the classic days of Hollywood, such trademarks were Bogart's toughness, John Wayne's reckless virility, Fonda's sensitive passion, Marilyn Monroe's soft, defenseless sexuality, Marlon Brando's vulnerable egotism, W.C. Fields's cynicism, Mae West's leering defiance, Grace Kelly's poise, and Clark Gable's cockiness. These were not "put on" personalities; they were intrinsic to their owners and vital to their owners' successes. The personalities of today's rising stars are more subtle, perhaps, but just as ingrained in their performances, even in varied characterizations.

You cannot create your personality—your stage personality—but you can liberate it. What are your personal characteristics? What do others see in you? Find out and let those characteristics come out. Do not worry about "your good features versus your bad features." Just have features. Don't be afraid to be different. Don't opt for the ordinary, for the timid, for the nice. Don't try to be what you think they want you to be. Don't worry about yourself. Be proud of yourself. *Like yourself.* If you don't, it's hard to see how somebody else will.

One other aspect of personality deserves some attention, one so obvious that most young actors completely ignore it: Does the director enjoy talking with you? There should be nothing surprising about this. Like everyone else, directors want to enjoy their work, and they would rather work with people they like than with people they don't like. Just as you do. There is an artistic component to this principle as well. Filmmaker William Bayer advises would-be directors "In the end the most important quality to look for in an actor may be rapport: are you going to be able to work with this actor on a basis of intimate friendship? When a film is shooting and the pressure is on, friendship and understanding may be the qualities that have most to do with failure or success."[14] While there is no assured way of generating that rapport, you should be able to recognize its importance, and open yourself up to it without feeling guilty. Perhaps it is safe to say that if you are the kind of person who combines vivacity with sensitivity, and sincerity with charm, then you might be the kind of person a director would choose for company—and for the Company.

"LOOKS" AND "TYPE"

Acting is one of the only professions (modeling is another) where looks count, and count *openly*. (In other professions looks may also count, but nobody will admit it.)

In acting, you can be hired for looks alone (particularly when you don't have to speak), and be hired largely on account of your physical "type" (fat and jolly, lean and hungry, nerdish and owly, as examples). Moreover, you can be *rejected* purely on the same grounds—you're the wrong race, sex, age, or size—grounds which, in almost any other field, would send the hiring officer to court.

But not in acting. Casting inequalities are endemic to the acting arts, and not necessarily because of racial prejudice or mean-spiritedness. The acting profession is, quite uniquely, an *unequal* opportunity employer, justified (by some) because the actor not only performs a role, he or she *depicts* a specific character, whose race and sex may be deemed—by the author, director, and/or producer—as crucial to the play's (or film's) meaning and impact, including its box office appeal. Most (though not all) directors would thus prefer (if not insist) that Henry V be played by a white male, and that Rose (in August Wilson's *Fences*) be played by a black woman. Cross-casting these parts over racial or gender lines could create audience confusion, unless the plays were substantially revised to fit with the cross-casting decisions.

The aspiring actor, therefore, must make a good hard study of prevailing type-casting realities before committing time and energy to tilting at windmills. *Most* casting in the professional theatre and in film and TV today is done, at least in part, by physical type. That's simply a fact.

Your physical type begins with your race and your sex, neither of which can ordinarily (unless you are a knighted English superstar) be altered by theatrical makeup. What this has meant in practical terms is that Caucasian males have had far more acting opportunities than other racial/gender groups, primarily because more parts have been written for them. Or have been *thought* to be written for them. Women, blacks, Hispanics, and other ethnic actors have had restricted opportunities. Although blacks, Hispanics, Asians, and Native Americans make up 22% of the U.S. population, they accounted for only 13% of the on-camera American network television performances in 1987—and then often as "exotics," rather than doctors, judges, private investigators, or romantic leads. The film *Platoon* was written for an Apache male lead, but "the film distribution people turned it around and said, 'Why don't you make this guy a white guy?'" according to Bob Morones, the film's casting director. And Willem Dafoe got the part.[15]

The burden of this discrimination is particularly ironic in the case of women, because women comprise up to three-fourths of the students enrolled in university and professional acting classes. Yet women receive only about *one-fourth to one-third* of the acting roles available professionally. This means that whatever the odds against male students' eventual acting success, the odds against females are close to ten times worse.   This is not mere discrimination on the part of male directors. Only about one-fourth to one-third of the *parts* in produced plays or films are written for women. Plays and films have in the past tended to be largely about men: national leaders, murderers, generals, attorneys, cops, athletes—real life roles, in other words, formerly dominated by the male sex. And though there is some countermovement on this front, discussed below, the male hegemony on dramatic material remains in practical force today.

Hence, while the status of women in the theatre has certainly improved since the Renaissance (when they weren't permitted to perform at all), it hasn't improved very much. In most repertory theatres, women ordinarily comprise no more than one-third of an acting company (in Shakespearean companies, it's less than one-fourth), and on television and films the ratio of women to men may be even slimmer. The Women's Conference Committee of the Screen Actors Guild (SAG) has pointed out that under SAG contracts male employment outnumbers female employment three-to-one—and a shocking five-to-one in the 35-45 age range, which contains the majority of starring roles. "At forty, women seem to drop off the face of the earth," says SAG spokesperson Norma Connolly.[16]   Even on television commercials men outnumber women two-to-one, and men also seize a gigantic 93% of the "voice-overs" (off-camera speaking roles).

Racial discrimination likewise remains in acting employment. Blacks and Hispanics, while widely visible in token roles, are underrepresented proportionally to their numbers in American society.

I am happy to report that this is beginning to change, partly because American life is beginning to change. American drama, for the first time, is recognizing this change, and is taking much greater interest in women and minorities. In the mid-1980s we see Tony and Pulitzer Prizes going to plays like *Crimes of the Heart*, *'Night Mother*, and *The Heidi Chronicles* (plays written by women about women), Charles Fuller's *A Soldier's Play* and August Wilson's *Fences* (both by and about blacks), and *M. Butterfly* (by a Chinese-American, about the Western view of Orientals). Likewise, 1980s Academy Awards to *Gandhi*, *Out of Africa*, *The Last Emperor*, *The Killing Fields*, and *Children of a Lesser God* have expanded our notion of the casting pool substantially.

The 33% of the roles women played in films and TV in 1987-1988 is at least a small improvement from the 31% noted in the last revision of this book (1982). And a new interest in nontraditional casting has led to the revision of film scripts to make male roles female, or at least gender-neutral: Sigourney Weaver's role in *Alien* was originally written for a man, Debra Winger's role in *Legal Eagles* was originally written for Bill Murray, and Whoopi Goldberg's role in *Burglar* was originally written for Bruce Willis. Goldberg's comment: "As an actor, you can play a speck of dust. Gender is not important." Director Hugh Wilson explains: "Warner Bros. initially had hoped that Whoopi would play a cameo role. When Bruce dropped out, she said, 'Hell, I'll do it.' Warner Bros. was very hot to have her. I think they would have changed Hamlet to a woman to get her."

Sometimes the script doesn't even need to be changed. The actress Linda Hunt won the 1983 supporting actress Oscar as the male Billy Kwan in *The Year of Living Dangerously*.

The legitimate stage is also opening up more for women: Neil Simon remade his *The Odd Couple* for Sally Struthers and Rita Moreno, and, with minor rewrites, Mary Tyler Moore and Luci Arnez went into the leading roles of *Whose Life Is It Anyway?* Black cast musicals—*Ain't Misbehavin'*, *The Wiz*, *Hello Dolly!*—have been common for years, sometimes (as in the last example) as second companies of previously all-white shows; and all-black or all-Asian versions of modern classics, such as *Long Day's Journey into Night*, *Three Sisters*, and *The Subject Was*

Roses, are becoming increasingly common in regional repertory and off-Broadway.

Finally, "nontraditional" casting conferences that deal with the casting of women and blacks in "generic" roles such as "a bank president" and "a doctor" are now held regularly on both coasts, and unions have begun to consider nondiscriminatory clauses in their general agreements with producers. Truly interracial and gender-neutral casting in classic plays is becoming increasingly common, as, for example, at the New York Public Theatre productions (for example, the 1988 *Coriolanus*). And, as women and minorities have moved significantly into power positions in life, their success has made them role models for the public, which translates into more diverse acting roles on the stage and screen. There are one black, one Hispanic, and three female lawyers in the cast of characters of TV's "L.A. Law," for example, reflecting the makeup of a firm that would not have been typical a generation ago. Such real-life changes have expanded by race and gender the casting pool of the "stage lawyer" role, which would once have been limited to white males.

"L.A. Law" also features a mentally disabled handyman, and while that part is played by a non-mentally disabled actor, the opportunities for performers with handicaps is increasing likewise, if a bit more slowly. Howie Seago, a deaf actor, stars in "Star Trek: The Next Generation." "I have made the work myself by my own perseverance," Seago reports. He actually proposed the deaf character to the producers himself, and they bought the idea.

Barbara Adside, who is legless, has performed on "Night Court," "Simon & Simon," "Fame," and "Cagney and Lacey." "They gave me every excuse in the book—from insurance to what-not—for why I would not be able to take acting classes or be on stage for theatrical productions," Adside says, adding that directors and producers "usually have a preconceived notion that somebody with a disability will slow down production." But Adside does everything, with or without prosthetic legs: It can be done.

Some of your physical characteristics, however, are more variable than sex, race, and physical handicap. Your weight, dress, health, posture, hair style, teeth, complexion, and grooming all allow you great latitude. How can an actor use these variables?

As with personality, there is no classic norm.

As with personality, the premium is on a specific, *memorable* and *definable* "look," and that look should be within a specific time-honored "type."

Types exist, and they exist today exactly as they did a hundred years ago: male and female "children," "younger leading men," "ingenues," "leading men," "leading women," "character men and comedians," and "character women and comediennes." There are subgroups, but these eight remain the basic ones. The *Players Directory*, which is a publication of photographs of all working actors in the Los Angeles area, and an invaluable tool in the casting process, divides actors into these categories for the convenience of producers. So does the *Players Guide*, a comparable publication in New York. In both books, if you aren't listed in the right category, you won't even be looked at.

> "Children" designates actors 12 years old and younger. "Preteens" are those from 13 to 15, and "teens" from 16 to 19. Ordinarily these character types are not involved in romantic affairs. On stage, anyway.

> "Ingenues" (girls) and "young leading men" are in the "first love" category. Usually they are in the early to mid-twenties and send off vibrations of youth, innocence, and charm.

> "Leading men" and "leading ladies" are, by contrast, wiser, more experienced lovers; glamorous, romantic, mature, sophisticated, in their mid-twenties to mid-forties and beyond.

> "Character men," "character women," "comedians," and "comediennes" are not romantic in a conventional sense. They are usually older, and their appearance is likely to be distinctive rather than attractive.

Notice that types are not defined solely by age, but also by a position on some sort of romantic/sexual scale. This is simply an accurate reading of the typing that is done in theatre and film casting. No one assumes that an unattractive character cannot be portrayed in a romantic role (as in *Rocky*). It is just that to do so is to cast deliberately against type, and such casting is done rarely except when a specific play or film calls for it. Since the time of Aristophanes, audiences have expected ingenues to be young and innocent, lovers to be beautiful and sensitive, and comics to be old and pudgy. Few casting directors wish to disappoint an audience.

It is important to find your type, if only to get yourself in the right chapter of the *Players Directory* or the *Players Guide*. More than that, your type will categorize you in the producer's mind. You are provided with a convenient label—a basis for comparison with other actors. You protest: You are an individual, not a type! Well, if you are Dustin Hoffman, you don't need a label. If you aren't, you have to start somewhere. Even "male" or "female" is a label, and you can be at least a little more specific than that.

You must decide whether you can play juveniles, for example. Either you can play 14-year-olds or you cannot. Perhaps you can do a passable job, of course, but can you do better than a *real* 14-year-old? If so, sign up, because producers hate to use real 14-year-olds if they can avoid it. (Hollywood studios really hate to use anybody younger than 18, because they can only work them for limited hours; also the studio must pay to have a tutor on the set. If you are 19 and can play 12, they will love you.)

And if you are going for romantic leads, particularly in film or television, you had better be very attractive. Indeed, *very* attractive. This may sound a bit unsettling, but it's simply a fact: Casting calls openly call for "gorgeous" or "beautiful" women—sometimes they even stipulate, quite shamelessly, "staggeringly beautiful." And the quest for male "hunks" whose very entrance will send the (largely female) soap opera audiences into a rapturous fantasy animates most daytime television casting directors.

Please don't underestimate the lengths to which TV and film casting directors will try to hunt out *extraordinarily* beautiful people, too. They are not just looking for collegiate charm and boyish/girlish attractiveness; they are seeking real knock-out sex appeal, an appeal that will make viewers leave one soap for another. A 1% change in the ratings can mean millions of dollars—not for you, but for somebody— and if a sexier smile or a bouncier bosom will generate that extra percent, that's where the casting will go. This doesn't get talked about much, but it's real. That's why you'll find all the ads in the trade papers for dentists and plastic surgeons. Tooth capping, porcelain laminate veneers, nose jobs, breast implants and reductions, chin tucks, and face lifts—all of these are commonly known in the world of actors. Mariel Hemingway's silicone implants, in conjunction with her *Star 80* role as a *Playboy* centerfold, even made national newswires. It is beyond the scope of this book to make surgical suggestions, but if you are planning to be up for straight romantic roles, you should at least take a close look at your teeth, and get some specialists to work with you on your hair and (for women, anyway) makeup.

You should clearly be a character actor or not. Weight and age have a lot to do with this: Character actors since Roman times have invariably been fat or old, if not fat and old, if not fat and old and ugly. You should surely know if you're fat or not, and you should be either fat or not fat—nothing in-between. Don't be neither fish nor fowl here. If you are ten or twenty pounds overweight, you are dead in the water. Either get your weight down to where it should be (and a bit lower in TV, since the tube will round you out a little) or gain forty more. And if you feel you are ugly, don't worry about trying to hide it. *Cultivate* it. Make it work for you. Use what you have to create a distinctive appearance. There is no "bad" appearance except a bland, character-less, typeless one.

What should you look like? That's your choice. Classic good looks, out for a while, are back in. Vanna White and Ted Danson could have made it in the 50s as easily as the 80s. Certain "nonclassic" looks "come in" from time to time: urban ethnic (Dustin Hoffman, Danny de Vito, John Malkovich, Al Pacino, Richard Dreyfuss, Woody Allen) came in strong in the late 60s and early 70s, and has been a particularly dominant look for leading men in recent years, while earthy frankness (Glenn Close, Meryl Streep, Sigourney Weaver, Whoopi Goldberg) seems to have largely replaced the bosomy voluptuousness that characterized most leading women of the past. All these "looks" can be cultivated, and in fact *have* been cultivated by most if not all of the actors who exhibit them.

The specifics of personal physical appearance are not individually important. What counts is the effect that your person and your "image" create, and the power of that effect, which should be enormous. If you are a leading man, you must appeal to women; if a woman, you must appeal to men. There are all kinds of ways of doing that, and for some it comes more naturally than for others. But you *can* do it if you're willing to devote some time, a little money, and a frankly self-critical attitude to the matter. The main difference between professional and amateur theatre auditions is the relative lack of concern most amateurs have over their personal appearance. Actually, this is a subtle form of arrogance: Let the Star of Bethlehem arise to shine over my hidden virtue. The folly of this proto-Messianic approach need not be discussed further.

Cultivate a *distinctive* appearance. Separate yourself from the rest of your friends. Find an exciting hairstyle for yourself, a natural one perhaps, but one that looks better on you than on anybody else, one that is not seen around too much. Dress distinctively. If you are a woman and you like going around in pinpoint shirts and slim leather coats, then get some that fit right, and some great accessories, and look terrific. The perfect jacket or sweater or slacks can make a nondescript male very descript indeed. They've got to remember you *somehow* when you leave the room—and they've got to remember your individual qualities. Extravagance and propriety are not worth a dram in this business, but distinction *in your own terms* is. Find yourself, and find in yourself a unique appearance that will intrigue others.

How about your weight? Unless you're bound and determined to be a character actor, get it down. And get your physical condition up to par—and better than par. Work out regularly. Most Americans are a bit overweight and a bit unfit, but most performers aren't, as most roles aren't written for chubby, flaccid actors. This is no accident. Characters in plays and films serve as role models to the public, and role models these days tend toward the lissome, lithe, strong, and supple. The physical demands of performing also reward those who are physically capable of meeting them, so exercise, diet, and get in *great* shape. This is particularly true if you have plans toward film and television, where the camera adds ten or fifteen pounds to you anyway. For young actors, heavy character roles are few. Take a look at the young people playing the three-line parts on television programs. These are the parts you will be going for if you're just starting out, and chances are they aren't heavyweights on the scales.

How do you *use* your appearance? It precedes you in every interview and every audition. No actor can begin to look for work without a set of photographs. They are your letters of introduction. (See the section on photographs in the next chapter. You may want to read it in conjunction with this one.) Your photographs must show just what your appearance must show: originality, vitality, distinctiveness. If you look like something out of a high school yearbook, the chances are that you will never be heard of again. And if you *are* like something out a high school yearbook, the same ignominy will result!

TRAINING AND EXPERIENCE

Every actor must have training and experience. No matter how naturally talented, attractive, sexy, and individual you are, you will flop in the audition if you don't know what to do. In the old days, actors without formal training were the rule. As Hermione Gingold once said, "I got all the schooling any actress needs. That is, I learned to write enough to sign contracts."[17] John Wayne bragged that he just learned his lines and went out and said them. Now, this sort of attitude has become very definitely the exception. Training in the art and craft of acting is a virtual necessity for a successful career, and if you *are* hired at first without training, as child actors or retired athletes often are in TV, you will need it before going much further.

What sort of training should you take? A virtual explosion over the past two decades in the area of arts education has spawned an extraordinary proliferation of drama schools and actor-training institutes, and the aspiring actor has many options.

University Training

A general college education, perhaps with a drama or theatre major, followed by a Master of Fine Arts degree from a qualified institute of higher learning, has clearly become the most desirable training base for professional *stage* actors, some of whom go on to become film/TV actors as well.

Stage acting, which remains based to a certain extent on the performer's sensitivity to literary values, acquaintanceship with political and social history, understanding of philosophical dichotomies, and general appreciation of art and culture, is favorably developed in an environment where classical as well as modern works are regularly analyzed, criticized, and performed. With more than 200 university drama departments now offering graduate acting degrees, the opportunity to receive advanced training, usually from instructors who have professional backgrounds and ongoing contacts, is available throughout the country. While it remains true, in the classic expression of New York Shakespeare Festival producer Joseph Papp, that "a Ph.D. won't get you through the turnstile of the IRT (the New York subway)," a strong college degree followed by advanced university actor training can give you that important entree to regional theatre stage work, and help you get from there to other media. "We are hard pressed even to *look* at someone without an Equity card or an M.F.A.," says Lee Shallat, former casting director for the South Coast Repertory Theatre, "and most of the other LORT (League of Resident Theatres) companies feel the same way."

Good college theatre departments provide preparation for more than just the regional or legitimate theatre these days. Most departments also offer some opportunity for film and TV acting as well. Even if they don't, stage training has become increasingly important in the film and TV casting worlds. "I love stage-trained actors; they are believable, they are funny, they know what to do," says Jeff Greenberg, casting director for "Cheers." "Stage training is the greatest training in the world," says Bobby Hoffman, casting director for the old "Laverne and Shirley" and "Mork and Mindy" shows, and now various Hollywood films.[18] "I think theatre people are just fantastic," concurs Lucy Grimes, casting director for daily television ("The Young and Restless"). "The minute I see they have some theatre training or I see them in a little theatre production, I try to use them," she continues. Susan Bedsow, formerly a producer of "As The World Turns" (and a former Broadway actress herself), adds that she and her casting colleagues prefer to cast college-trained stage actors and, even beyond that, *classically* trained stage actors, in soap operas, because such actors are more readily able to create an ongoing character in depth. Nicholas Walker, cast right out of college as a leading performer in the daytime series "The Doctors," now on "The Young and the Restless," "trained" for his role by playing the title roles in college productions of *Hamlet*, *Richard III*, *Peer Gynt*, and *The Philanthropist*. He had never been on camera until his successful NBC screen test. Powers Boothe, the Emmy-winning film and television actor, spent his first six years after college (Southwest Texas State University, plus graduate work at Southern Methodist University) playing Shakespeare in Oregon and other classic roles at the Pacific Conservatory of the Performing Arts. "I wouldn't trade that for anything," observes Boothe. "If you can accomplish all the necessary things in Shakespeare with the language and the poetry—and can make it real—then you must know your craft." This is becoming more and more the rule throughout the acting media. Actors who previously hid their university credentials behind a rock and pretended that Shakespeare was a Houston shortstop now brag about their academic and classical credits in their "Who's in the Cast" program write-ups and in their capsule biographies in popular magazines.

The "academicization" of the acting arts is a relatively new phenomenon. Much of it has been connected with the great growth in nonprofit legitimate theatre. Today there are over 200 such theatres, while only about a dozen existed before 1960. Nonprofit theatres often have academic roots; many if not most of them were formed by the faculties of, or graduates from, strong M.F.A. programs. But the film and TV worlds are also now staffed and headed, to a greater degree than ever before, by college-trained men and women. Even Hollywood agents these days more often than not have university degrees, although they rarely post their diplomas on their office walls.

There are many ramifications of this evolving relationship between academic and professional worlds. For many years a national collegiate drama festival has been held in Washington, D.C., offering wide recognition to college actors through the Irene Ryan acting award. Many college-connected professional theatres, some operating in the summertime and some during the school year, now provide "halfway" employment situations where students can work with professionals. Apprenticeships and internships now connect several university drama departments with nearby or on-campus professional companies, and offer seasonal opportunities for students to act with, study with, and rub elbows with professional actors on a regular basis. Sometimes even union membership credits can be obtained in the process. And a provision by the Screen Actors Guild provides that the fine levied against producers for hiring nonunion talent can be waived, and the actor allowed into the union, if the actor can present evidence of sufficient training, such as an M.F.A. degree, so as "to qualify for a career as a professional actor." All these factors favor university training as a base for the emerging actor's career.

But not all is wonderful in university drama departments, and there are several things you must watch out for.

Perhaps the most important thing is that the university environment, even under the best circumstances, is an amateur one—and sometimes it is amateurish as well. Universities have a disproportionate number of young people, and university directors often cast young people in older roles. This can create a resigned attitude with regard to casting standards: the production will aspire only to a minimal level of competence, a level that is "all that can be achieved under the circumstances." There is no harm in this unless it drags down your *own* standards, which, unfortunately, it is likely to do. Audiences in the professional theatre are not as indulgent of circumstances, and not as amused by the often-affected performances of adolescents as aged kings, queens, and master builders. Performing such roles may not be all that good for you, either.

In addition, there is a back-patting coziness in many drama departments that can lull student actors into a false sense of security, preventing them from developing their craft in a disciplined manner, and encouraging them to rest on yet ill-deserved laurels. Many students come to New York with their M.F.A.'s in hand and glowing reviews in their portfolio, but with slender skills, sketchily developed and only casually tested against a too-easily-won campus popularity.

There are also many campus drama instructors, academically trained, who (consciously or unconsciously) resent the professional theatre world; and there are others, professionally experienced, who have fled the professional world in anger or bitterness. Both can badly misrepresent the profession.

And finally, there are a few programs that are simply bad, out of touch with the profession, professing to teach what they know nothing about.

How should you pick a good college or graduate drama school? How do you avoid a hopelessly antiquated or inadequate one? Ask around, of course, and get recommendations from teachers, school counselors, and professional actors and directors. Look at the catalogues of major universities. No one would quarrel with the notion that the Yale Drama School in New Haven, and the Juilliard School in New York are the most celebrated academic acting schools in the country, and have produced a great share of our leading actors, but there are many other outstanding institutions.

Some, but by no means all, of the best departments are in the University/Resident Theatre Association, which holds collective auditions for admission. Others advertise in journals: *American Theatre, The Drama Review*, and *Theatre Journal*, most prominently. Books that list schools are noted in the appendix at the back of this book. If you're interested in a drama school, read the ads, read the catalogues in your library, and write to the schools that interest you. *Visit* the three or four departments that seem most suitable to your interest and finances. *Write* to the departments that interest you and let them know you're coming. Ask to *see* both faculty-directed and student-directed productions, if that can be arranged. Ask to visit an acting class. Hang around the bulletin board—there is *always* a bulletin board—and talk to the students you see there. Try to get the inside picture. Wherever you will go, you'll be there for a long while, so get active in your search. Find out as much as you can before committing your time and money.

Some things to look for in choosing a theatre school:

- A faculty with *professional experience*. At least some of the faculty in acting should be professional actors, or should have been professional actors, preferably in a variety of acting media.

- A faculty *presently involved* in professional theatre; or a program with active apprenticeships in professional theatre. You want to be taught up-to-date techniques, and you want to work with people who have professional contacts themselves.

- An *organized plan* for the training of actors. A fine acting program is not merely a collection of fine actors revealing the secrets of their craft. A good program has a working methodology, or pedagogy, with various courses directly feeding into each other so that you will graduate with integrated and comprehensive training, not just a mish-mash of information and critiques.

- *Proximity* to ongoing professional theatre activity. This means within commuting distance of New York or Los Angeles, or at least near a city (or cities) with more than one resident professional company. You should have the opportunity to view professional work at more than one theatre, and with frequency, and to see it in relation to your own work.

- *Facilities, staff, and budgets* sufficient to ensure quality work at all levels. This does not mean that the college or university must boast a battery of multimodal theatres with computer lightboards and hydraulic stages (although some do). It does mean that works put on by the department must be respectable, and not prefaced by bundles of apologies or disclaimers. It also means a hardworking and energetic staff, willing to put in time with you.

- *Good student morale.* Drama students traditionally gripe to each other, yet put on shining faces to outsiders. Both behaviors indicate healthy morale. Watch out for any program where the students are unwarrantedly complacent or openly bitter.

- Opportunities to study *dance* and *voice* (singing) as well as acting. Stage actors particularly should seek as much training in music theatre as possible because more and more contemporary stage plays demand musical abilities. Since versatility is important for every stage actor, you should find and take every opportunity to enlarge your performing repertoire. Check also for opportunities to learn stage combat, mime, period movement, and audition technique.

- Opportunities to study *classical* acting. You may not think Shakespeare is your metier, but you should study it anyhow. The training may come in handy five years down the road, and besides, you might discover a talent you never imagined you possessed. Most LORT theatres do regular productions of the classics, at least once a year. Your ability to perfom Shakespeare or Molière will certainly be a strong point in your favor when you compete for an apprenticeship or for a paid position with these companies.

- Opportunities to work *on camera*. Some universities have videotape facilities or complete TV studios where you can learn to work on camera, and study how to hit your marks while playing a scene. You *can* learn this later, but a school that provides such opportunities gives you a chance to get a jump on the competition.

- *Superior work*. Above all, be sure the school productions look good. The level of acting should be at your level or better. Don't ever go to a school because you think you'll have an easy chance to walk off with the starring roles there. You want the *best* possible school, the *best* possible teachers, and the *best* possible fellow students. You might as well start getting used to high-level competition; you'll face it from now on.

A final word about college: While you're there, don't waste your time. Study, of course, all the theatre you can. Learn to sing and dance—learn ballet, tap, and jazz. Learn to fence. Study literature, history, psychology, politics, economics, philosophy. These things will not only feed your art, they will feed you. As actress Suzanne Pleshette says, "Make sure you have a real life, other interests, things that fill you, because if you only live when you're working, you lead a very shallow existence and you have very little to bring back to the work."[19] Actors these days are smart and they are active; they branch into writing and directing, they engage in politics, they teach. As the late Duncan Ross, when artistic director of the Seattle Repertory Theatre, said, "There is no such thing as a good actor who is unintelligent." Train, yes, but also *learn*: Use, explore, and expand your mind.

Commercial Training

Commercial training refers to a collection of schools and teachers, mainly in New York and Los Angeles, that teach acting (and often related theatre disciplines) for set fees. These institutions and individuals are not affiliated with universities, and do not ordinarily offer subjects unrelated to theatre.

The number of commercial acting schools has increased tremendously in the past decade. A Los Angeles directory lists several dozen in that city alone (*The Acting Coaches and Teachers Association Directory*); in New York more than forty teachers and schools advertise weekly in the trade magazines *Backstage* and *Show Business*. See the appendix for the bookstores selling these publications.

Commercial school and teachers vary enormously in the nature of their offerings and in the quality of their instruction. Some are full drama schools, providing comprehensive theatre education. Others are schools devoted to a single teacher's method of self-expression. Others are specialized academies for certain skills: camera acting, TV commercials, improvisation, stage speech, comedy, singing, dance, audition technique, and the like. Many schools and teachers offer a variety of courses and classes; including, usually, a basic acting sequence plus a variety of specialized workshops. Naturally the comprehensive schools are geared to the student without prior dramatic training, while the independent teachers and class offerings are more suitable to the university-trained actor located in New York or Los Angeles. Specialized classes provide a source of continuing education for actors, and are very much part of the actor's life, even after roles start coming in. Internationally known actors frequently show up in acting classes in New York and Hollywood to refresh their skills and learn new ones.

Finding a commercial class is tricky because, unlike universities and colleges, there is no system of regular outside accreditation, and commercial schools go in and out of business—sometimes as often as the teachers go in and out of acting roles. Look at the ads, get recommendations, interview the directors, and ask to audit a class. Talk to current students. Remember, commercial acting classes live through your tuition, and their advertisements and recruitment techniques are designed to make you *think* the classes are indispensable to your future. Beware of *any* acting teachers who imply that studying with them guarantees professional employment; this is actually *illegal* in California, although it hasn't prevented hundreds of innuendos to that effect from being widely circulated by too-hungry instructors. Watch out also for acting classes that require you to pay for several months in advance, or to pay for management services, photographs, or for separate showcases to which "important casting directors" (always unnamed) will be invited. (Many are invited, but few will come.) These are almost all shams. The best courses and teachers are fair in their prices, frank in their advertising, honest in their evaluation of your potential, and open and above board in their registration and tuition policies. Don't be afraid to ask questions and don't be willing to accept less than complete answers.

Who should study at commercial schools? Probably just about everybody. The main advantage of the commercial school is that it is right in the midst of professional activity, it is run by professionals with "real world" values dominating every classroom exercise and discussion, and your fellow students will be like-minded professional aspirants. Full training programs, such as the Neighborhood Playhouse School of the Theatre in New York, are well designed for the high school graduate, and intensive month-by-month programs, such as the HB Studio in New York (run by husband and wife team Herbert Berghof and Uta Hagen) and the Film Actors' Workshop in Hollywood (run by CBS producer Tony Barr) are excellent for professional training beyond the academy or the M.F.A. Many of these schools will begin by "retraining" you—suggesting (sometimes quite fervidly) that you "unlearn" your collegiate technique in favor of the teacher's style. Go along with it. You never really unlearn anything anyway, and it's what you *do* learn that's going to count.

When you get into a professional class, as you should as soon as you hit New York or Los Angeles, get right to work, and work hard. Commercial schools do not have grades or examinations; there is no motivation for study except your own drive to learn. Hard work and energy, not money, is your main investment. You will get out of these classes precisely what you put into them—a cliché perhaps, but one that is never so true as in an acting class. Meet the other people in the class and get to know them; they will be your first contacts in the professional world that you wish to enter.

Apprenticeships

Apprenticeship programs are a third possible training ground for actors, and the best of these offer excellent opportunities for professional development—when you can get them.

Apprenticeships (or internships, as they are sometimes called) put you in direct daily contact with working professionals, and usually have you working side by side with them. Some offer acting classes in addition, and some even offer credits toward union membership under Equity's Membership Candidate program. You will ordinarily pay for room and board, and you may pay a tuition fee as well, although in some cases these may be negotiated if the company wants you and your skills badly enough.

The best apprenticeships are at those LORT theatres that offer seasonal and year-round programs. Some of these apprenticeships are operated in conjunction with university drama departments, such as the joint programs of the Yale Drama School with the Yale Repertory Theatre, or of Florida State University with the Asolo Theatre. A LORT theatre apprenticeship can provide you with the fifty weeks of work necessary to qualify for an Equity card (see the section on unions in the next chapter), as well as a sound education in professional theatre practice. Summer theatre programs at outstanding resident stock theatres, such as Williamstown and Stockbridge in Massachusetts, are also great training grounds for professional actors, as has been demonstrated over past decades. You can find information about apprenticeships through summer theatre publications (see the appendix), through the University/Resident Theatre Association, and by writing directly to professional theatre companies that you know have such programs, or that you think might be interested in creating one.

A Word of Caution

One final cautionary word about preprofessional training: It can be overdone. College, acting classes, and the local community theatre can be very comfortable places. A lovely security envelops you: You are known, liked, respected, and well reviewed by the locals and by your teachers. But check your goals. If you want to move on, you had better go when you are ready rather than hang around merely because it is safe. Recognize the point of stagnation when the competition gets soft. There are actors who become so devoted to a favorite drama school or drama teacher that they study for eight or ten years without going to a single audition, on the grounds that they are "not ready." The "professional student" is really psychologically aberrant. Recognize this trait in yourself, if it exists, and fight it. When you are ready to take the plunge, take it. The proper time is something only you can decide upon.

CONTACTS

Here we are. Contacts are the nemesis of the young unknown actor. You can whine, gripe, yell, and complain about it, but contacts are important—*vital*—in getting jobs in the theatre. But do not just give up on this account: *Think.* What does the term "contacts" actually mean?

Contacts are the people you know and who know you. Switch sides for a moment. If you were casting a play in a hurry and knew that Harry was "just right" for the role, wouldn't you call Harry and ask him to audition? Would you really search through the drama classes at Amalgamated State University to find out if there were somebody else as good? No. You would call Harry and say, "Harry, I've got a part that's just right for you." And Harry would come over and read it, and if you liked his reading you would cast him in the role. It's not that you owe Harry a favor, but you like Harry, you envision Harry doing the part, and you can settle the matter in a quick, friendly way. Well, maybe you are the one in a thousand who wouldn't call Harry, but the other 999 are in New York and Hollywood casting offices right now. You can either moan about it or work to become Harry. The choice is yours.

There is nothing mysterious about "contacts," and it is fruitless to play sour grapes and say "I can't get anywhere because I don't have any pull." Of course you don't, but neither does anybody else just starting out. It is not as though your competition all went to school with Tom Cruise or swam in Glenn Close's pool. Everybody, or almost everybody, starts off just as unknown and unwanted as you. If you don't have contacts, you just have to develop some. It is as simple as that.

But wait a minute, you say. You don't *accept* that "It's who you know, not what you know." You want to make it "on your own." Well, what does *that* mean? That you will be discovered? Where? In your acting class? Singing in the shower? The fact is that NOBODY ever makes it on his or her "own." It always takes *somebody else*, and that somebody else is your contact.

This is no time to play around with semantics. Getting jobs in theatre involves getting people to know you and know your work. These people are your contacts, and if you are good enough, and develop enough of them, one of them will pay off for you. And then it doesn't matter if you got introduced because he was your uncle's cousin or your drama teacher's drama teacher. Someone sees you, likes you, and hires you. How else do you expect it to happen?

Most hirings in the theatre and film world are, in fact, done among a network of acquaintances and friends—not *all* of it, but *most* of it. Why? Because, all else being equal (and most of the time, all else *is* equal), directors and producers prefer to work with actors they have worked with before over those they have never seen. And they would rather see people they know than total strangers. You have to break into the network, and you have to get contacts.

And now, who said you have no contacts? *Everybody you know* is a potential contact. The actor in the community play with you might next year be producing a film; your college drama instructor might be directing a play; your aunt might have a friend who has just written a TV show. It is to your advantage to get to know people in the business. Who knows what they might be doing in a month or so? Many actors mail postcards to everyone they know every four to six months, just to stay in the network. Such "networking" (yes, it's now a verb) is not presumptuous: It is appreciated, and it works.

The important contacts you presumably do not know yet, but you will. Every time you audition you meet at least one. At every interview you meet secretaries, directors, and other actors. These meetings can be forgotten in an instant, but if you are personable and they are intrigued by you, a contact is made. You don't have to be pushy. Phony friendliness and phony friends are the most loathsome aspect of show business, and it is easy to completely misplay your hand in this way. Theatre people are the worst name-droppers in the world and "Oh, he's a good friend of mine," becomes a line that is too frequently applied to a person met once five years ago. But you can build your real network of contacts—the people who know you and know your work—by simply and modestly finding ways to keep your friends aware of you. And you can keep aware of *them*, by writing down in a little black book the names of everyone you meet, so that the next time you see them you can remember their names and what they do.

Remember these fundamental principles about contacts:

- No *one* contact is going to make it for you, and the fact that somebody else knows somebody important is not going to make it for him or her, either. Everyone you know can help you, and themselves, by trading information, tips, advice, and, ultimately, offers of employment.

- People you have known for years and who have subsequently "made it" may not help you out at all. That is not just because success has made them indifferent to their old pals. Many genuinely try to follow the suggestion of Edith Piaf, who said that when you reach the top you should throw the ladder back down for everybody else. But your newly arrived friends are not as secure as they seem. In fact, they are in a particularly vulnerable position. Even if they can help you, they may not want to risk suggesting you to *their* higher-ups, fearing that if you fail, they'll fall. Beyond this, they may question their earlier evaluation of you now that they have new surroundings and a new perspective. They would rather you made it on your own—then they could be *sure*. This is small comfort, of course, but you will probably have to live with it.

- Contacts may not look like contacts. The mousy-looking man hanging around backstage might just be getting ready to film *Rocky X*, and is looking you over for a part. Be yourself and make friends; it can't hurt you.

- Contacts may not *act* like contacts. People who give out jobs in show business are so besieged they frequently hide the fact behind a veil of feigned clumsiness and innocence. Play along.

- All kinds of people will *tell* you that they are contacts. They're probably not. Maybe they are just nice and want to help, and maybe they are after you for other reasons. Some just like to sound important. Treat everybody the same, and stay a bit skeptical.

A word about sleeping with the producer. If you are a talented, personable, charming, and sexy person, there will be all sorts of people interested in casting you. And there will also be all sorts of people interested in going to bed with you. But these will quite possibly not be the same people.

A cartoon that used to hang outside the Screen Gems casting office window shows a young girl dressing in a bedroom and calling to an older man, "Now, when are you going to make me a star?" The older man is in the next room, smiling and cutting her a paper star.

Let's not be prudish, though. It is illogical to assume that if the casting director is your intimate he or she won't be working a little harder for you than for others who come in for interviews. It is equally obvious that if your bed partner is a studio executive, all things are not going to be equal when it comes to casting the next show. You've already read about the strings pulled to get a well-bedded actress into *The Steagle*, but the follow-up is that once shooting was underway the lady was fired, and the net result was much poorer for her than if she had not been hired in the first place. The point is that nobody gets a job *simply* by going from one studio bed or office couch to another. No producer makes that kind of deal; too much money is at stake, and too many people are ready to axe *him* if you are not good enough. And, quite frankly, there's a lot of sex available for a lot less (financial) risk. If you go to bed with anybody, don't expect anything but a good time.

In fact, the sexual politics of the acting industries are infinitely more subtle and fascinating than the old clichés about Broadway casting couches and Hollywood moguls chasing starlets through the back lot. Of course, there are producers, agents, and conglomerate accountants whose fantasies ignite when they contemplate the power they have and the oversupply of beautiful young people subject to that power. One casting director resigned because, he said, he was tired of pimping for his producer. But sexual trade-offs are rarely proposed directly, and they are rarely if ever explicit. Indeed, with new government regulations on sexual harassment, they are becoming close to impossible. Casting director Mike Fenton (*Bad News Bears*), who keeps a woman assistant at his side at all times, reports, "You never, never interview a woman in anything other than a very open situation." Perhaps, as it is often said, there is no more sexual dealing in show business than in the washing machine business or any other business, only it is simply more gossiped about in the general news media. An example comes to mind of one young, uninhibited, and absolutely beautiful young actress who went out on seventy-five interviews in her first year in Hollywood without receiving a single overt pass. She did receive a few roles and performed well in them. "The passes come after you're hired," she said. She also related the adventure of a competitor who came to a screen test wearing the tiniest miniskirt and no underwear. Not only did this fail to get her the part, but the infuriated (and family-oriented) director kicked her off the lot.

COMMITMENT AND WILL TO SUCCEED

Your power supply is your sense of commitment and your will to succeed. They will keep you going despite the thousand and one ego reversals you are bound to encounter. As a young, professional actor explains, the greatest danger you face is going "DEAF—depressed, envious, aching, and frustrated." It is your commitment and sheer persistence that will vanquish DEAFness if anything can, that will keep you going through poverty and loneliness, when your friends are marrying and having kids and making money and you are eating out of cans on the Lower East Side waiting for your ship to come in. You must continue to hang in there, to train yourself, to get information, to develop contacts. To do all these things, you must have an overwhelming desire for success. It is often said that the people who make it in the theatre are simply those who want it badly enough.

It is not necessary to step on other people's toes, to do zany things that draw attention to yourself, or to alienate friends, relatives, and competitors in your quest for success. But quest for it you must. Getting started in theatre means *initiating* actions: getting on the telephone and on the pavement, looking up people, calling on strangers, getting to places at 6 A.M. and waiting around for three hours—all sorts of indelicate and unappetizing tasks. It also means weeks, months, even years of frustration, failure, defeat, and simple boredom. It means sitting around waiting for the telephone to ring when it has not rung in months. These things are at best unpleasant and at worst may lead you to the brink of suicidal depression. Only a massive will to succeed will overcome them. The commitment must be strong, persistent, and all-encompassing. All sorts of personal sacrifices must be assumed.

Nobody knows how long it will take to "make" you an actor. It is best to set yourself some sort of time schedule—most actors do. Three years is an average allotment, three years after the first day that you say to yourself, "I am now an actor, and I'm available for work." Three years from the day you hit the pavements, the studios, the agencies—from the day you decide that whatever you are doing, you will drop it to get the first job.

From that day on, you scrimp on money for gifts, for food, for furniture, for an apartment. You spend money on pictures, a telephone service, resumes, acting classes, membership in a health club, and some good clothes for auditions. You get the sleep you need and the medication and exercise you need; you're going to have to be ready to look terrific on an hour's notice any day of the week. You direct your time, your money, and your energy to two things: learning acting and getting work. Whatever is left over goes to less important things like your social life or your marriage. Yes, less important. If you aren't 100% committed to your career, you will be passed over by someone who is.

And if you succeed, you still haven't "made it." "Listen, my dear," the late actress Ruth Gordon said to her *Harold and Maude* co-star Bud Cort, "you *never* make it. I'm on that phone twelve hours a day. I make it happen for myself, you're gonna make it happen for yourself. No one makes it."[20]   An actor never relaxes, because an actor—even a star—is always out of work, always looking for the next job. "You can't hang onto your laurels," said veteran James Earl Jones, discussing his profession. "Actors do not have choices, do not have claims, just because they are considered stars. I'm a troubadour, going from castle to castle looking for an open door through which to walk and sing for my supper. That's the way it is; it never changes."

But there's nothing grim about this. A committed attitude, such as that personified by Ruth Gordon and James Earl Jones, carries with it something more than just a pragmatic advantage in selling yourself on the job market. Exciting people are committed people—in art, in politics, or in life. And it is to your advantage to be exciting.

So be dedicated. It will offend the weak, but it will inspire others. A life of dedication (to your art, hopefully, but even to yourself) is fulfilling; it galvanizes your talents and directs your energies. It characterizes all great artists of all times. As Bernard Shaw wrote:

> This is the true joy in life, the being used for a purpose recognized by yourself as a mighty one: the being thoroughly worn out before you are thrown on the scrap heap, the being a force of Nature instead of a feverish selfish little clod of ailments and grievances, complaining that the world will not devote itself to making you happy.[21]

So live as if you meant it, and become an artist in the same way. This involves a little presumptuous egotism; flow with it. Michelangelo, Beethoven, Bernhardt, Heifetz, Toscanini, Machiavelli, Aeschylus: All great artists have been persons of great dedication and temperament, persons who have sacrificed easy-going pleasantness to the drive for perfection that has welled up inside them. If you are determined to make it as an actor, you are living life at high stakes anyway. You might as well go all the way with it.

ATTITUDE, DISCIPLINE, AND CAPACITY FOR PSYCHOLOGICAL ADJUSTMENT

How crippling are the comments, "He has a bad attitude!" or "She's undisciplined." They keep talented performers out of work and get them places on informal, rumor-fed blacklists that they may not truly deserve. The slightest whisper, from one associate producer to another, that "we've got enough problems in this show without dealing with *hers!*" is frequently the last exchange before "Thanks very much, dear. We'll be in touch with you if anything comes up."

It may be desirable to be daffy, but it is death to be genuinely crazy, or have casting people think you are. Crazy people are hard to contact, don't show up on time, forget their lines and their blocking, annoy other actors, antagonize directors, defy wardrobers, and in general are far more trouble than they are worth. If you are crazy, hide it. If you aren't, please don't pretend to be.

But mental health means more than merely being on the near side of psychosis. To be relatively stable, well-balanced, gregarious, and sensitive to the plights of others is a valuable asset. But there are more specific ways in which your attitude can work for you or against you.

Perhaps the worst attitude—the most destructive one—that appears commonly in young actors is the one that says, "I'm waiting to be discovered." This is a complex neurosis, and its effects are virtually fatal. Actors with this attitude are afraid of trying, afraid of looking foolish, afraid of failing. They never contact agents, never set up interviews, and never discuss career plans or goals with anyone but close friends. Considering self-promotion callous, these actors dedicate their time to perfecting some small aspect of their craft. Secretly, such actors hope that some unknown benefactor will find them in their hidden places of work and sign them to giant film contracts. But they will never take the initiative because that would soil their "purity."

One must beware of this attitude because it masks itself under seemingly noble forms. Basically it is simple fear. It is also egotism: the belief that one's own talent is so obvious that it need only be seen once to be instantly appreciated and called into demand. It is also romanticism: no Hollywood movie about the birth of a star has ever shown the aspirant plowing through the yellow pages or passing hours in the waiting rooms of an agent's office. The heroine has been discovered by the producer who visits the little summer stock theatre, or has been an understudy who is called on at the last moment to replace the aging star. The fact is that it takes plain work to get work in return, and *you* must go out and do the work because nobody is going to do it for you.

Another attitude that will hurt you if you overplay it is obvious disdain for the role, play, or medium for which you are auditioning. For example, it is not hard to find dozens of people working on a television show that will grumble about its lack of artistic integrity. Be careful about jumping on this particular bandwagon. Most people working in the theatre, films, or television *like* what they are doing, at least while they're doing it. At the very least they persuade themselves they like doing it. You may never watch a TV show yourself, but if you are reading for "Night Court," it won't help you to take a superior attitude to the art of television or to the premises of the program. The producers, directors, and actors are all intelligent, sensitive people They probably have pride in what they are doing, even if they don't always act like it. To mock the show mocks them, so don't be led into following their self-deprecating remarks. Every director would prefer to cast an actor who will appreciate the role, the play, and the medium.

Discipline is a primary ingredient in the professional actor's attitude. In fact, discipline is usually considered the chief distinction between the amateur and the professional. Good colleges, commercial schools, and community theatres insist on it, but these are in a minority. Discipline means that for the entire period between your first call and your dismissal you are concentrating on your tasks as an actor to the exclusion of everything else. It means you are always on time or early for every call: *not just usually, but always.* There is absolutely no reason for an actor to be even one minute late to a single audition, rehearsal, or makeup call—whether you're a star or an extra. As Maureen Stapleton puts it, "Actors are the only people, good or bad, hot or cold, who show up on time."

Promptness means you are always there and ready to do what you are asked, and that all your acting instruments—voice, body, imagination, and intelligence—are at the disposal of the director every moment you are on call.

Not that it is always easy to see this in a professional situation. If you have the chance to watch the taping of a television show you will see actors lounging around, talking to each other, joking on the set, drinking coffee, dropping lines during takes, and generally exhibiting an air of nonchalance. What you will also observe, however, is the immediate attention that the director can command, and how within a matter of five seconds twenty-five people will snap into total concentration and readiness. The nonchalance is necessary relaxation, but it is superficial. These are professionals, conditioned like flight crews to an ever-ready professional alertness. Until you are experienced enough to have one eye always open to the job at hand, concentrate fully on what you are doing. If you don't, you might find yourself still laughing at some joke by the coffeepot, while everybody else has suddenly reappeared on the set and the director is calling your name. In a rage.

Artistic temperament can be a drive for perfection and impatience with inefficiency, or it can mask your inexperience and demonstrate your lack of discipline. It's obviously to your advantage to be easy to work with. "The reason I will use actors from last year's festival is that I know I can work with them," said former California Shakespeare Festival artistic director Mark Lamos. "I don't care for temperament at all. I don't need egos. I want real pros."[22]

Discipline includes a willingness to take direction. No good director will become offended or irritated by genuine questions or discussion about blocking, emphasis, or motivation, but continual complaints such as "It doesn't feel right," particularly when they are obviously meant to cover insecurity, drive directors up the wall and may land you out of a job—sometimes right then and there. Among professionals, an inability to take direction may become your most talked-about liability, and unless you are sure that your presence in the play or film will draw thousands of paying spectators, you cannot afford that reputation.

The major cliché in director-actor hassles may be mentioned here, although if you have been in any theatre in America you have already heard it. That is when the "old school" director (say, George Abbot) tells the "method" actor (say, Marlon Brando) to cross left, and the actor mulls it over and asks, "What's my motivation?" "Your paycheck!" retorts the director. Nothing in today's theatre is that cut and dried, however. The director-actor relationship must be a balanced one, and both artists must genuinely desire to work well together for it to succeed. Obviously, since you are the one who is starting out, you have to do your part *plus*, despite possible disagreements.

In short, your attitude should be positive and infectious. You like the part, you like the play, you like the medium, you like the director and the direction, and you want like hell to do it and do it well. Nobody ever really gets offended at an actor who is genuinely eager, unless that eagerness pushes everybody else off the set. No director is offended by an actor, for example, who reads the play before auditions and memorizes half-a-dozen roles, and who communicates the genuine feeling that he will work like crazy if he gets the part; professional theatre art, behind the scenes, isn't at all casual. While you must never cross over the line by noisily and obsequiously flattering the producers, a clear tone of enthusiasm for the project is bound to be in your favor, and notes of ironic weariness or indifference to it will work powerfully (albeit silently) against you.

FREEDOM FROM ENTANGLEMENTS
AND INHIBITIONS

Freedom is complex and it does not exist in the absolute. Everyone is bound by restraints: practical, financial, social, and mental. Success in the pursuit of an acting career requires minimizing, not utterly eliminating, these restraints.

An actor must be free to audition for roles and to accept employment when and where it is offered. The important job offer can come at an awkward time (in the archetypal Hollywood story it always comes as the actor is about to leave on a honeymoon) and can send you to an inconvenient location. You must be free to accept it, however.

Commitment to an acting career means frequent (or at least occasional) slacking-off on other commitments, particularly those to husbands and wives, babies, friends, parents, outside employers, and teachers. Obviously it is better if you can arrange your priority of commitments in such a way that your career plans may proceed unhindered.

Naturally there will be some conflicts of interest here. You are an actor, but you are also a human being in a society, and you have friends, family, and all sorts of people whose plans and whose feelings will affect yours. After all, there are 8,760 hours in a year, and even a fully employed actor will spend 7,000 of them away from the set; if you have alienated all your friends just to be at the beck and call of every agent and producer in the business, you are apt to spend a lot of lonely hours by the TV set.

The only thing you can do is to come completely to grips with the nature of the business you are trying to enter and make certain that people who may depend on you are aware of it, too—and are also sympathetic to your ambitions. They may not be. Many actors who know the score vow never to marry another actor. An actor is rarely the model wife or husband of whom Dear Abby would be proud. As an actor, you will be subject to an ever-changing, unpredictable schedule; you will be on call for location work in Yugoslavia or New Haven while your spouse is taking care of the house and babies; you will be facing the terrific frustration of looking for parts and breaks in an industry where unemployment is routine; you will be sacrificing much of your income for classes and workshops and hundreds of photos and postcards of your lovely self; and finally, when you do start to get work, you will be deeply involved in the emotional crises, love affairs, and strange psychologies of the characters you are given to play. Face it: You're no prize. And face realistically the trials your relationship will inevitably endure.

Should an actor get married at all? Well, it is far beyond the scope of this little book to recommend one way or the other, and it is also doubtful that any recommendation here would be very seriously considered anyway. However, it is obvious that marriage *can* become a serious entanglement to a stage or film career if both of you fail to understand what you are getting into. If you marry without such an understanding, either you will completely frustrate your spouse and your marriage will end up in ruins, or you will frustrate yourself and your career will end up in ruins. You are no doubt already aware that the acting profession has a ridiculously high divorce rate. For some people it is an either/or situation. In a candid interview, Shelley Winters explained, "You see, honey, you've got to really make a choice in life. It's either a good role or a good marriage . . . I guess I love working more than being married . . . so I gave up this great guy for this great role."[23] And so it goes: You probably *can't* have everything.

And there's the financial matter. You can't be sure of supporting anyone, including yourself. Ideally, a young actor should marry only if he or she is rich or working, or marrying someone else who is. And an actor should marry only someone who understands the rigors of the career. Having said this, we rest our case. There are, after all, more than pragmatic considerations in this matter.

There are other entanglements besides marriage, of course. Some are financial, some emotional. You may be unwilling or unable to move around, to work with certain kinds of people, or to play certain kinds of parts. You may object to undressing in front of the camera (or an audience), or performing in a way you find undignified. There is a line you must draw for yourself here, but naturally the lower that line (that is, the fewer your inhibitions) the more "available" you are. Insofar as that line now must be drawn to include or exclude doing nude scenes (which occur in numerous movies), you will have to be prepared to define your views on this issue if you plan to work in films. There is, however, one "inhibition" that is known as "taste." An actor *must* be inhibited from doing things that are tasteless and unrewarding. Performing in the nude for a major art film and for a one-day stag movie obviously have different values, both as a creative act and as a step in your professional career. A young actor who is 100% available to do a blue film for a $100 fee may find himself or herself unusable for anything *but* that in the future. As Georgina Spelvin, the undraped star of *The Devil in Miss Jones* said recently, "Be aware, girls, if you make the choice to go into explicit pictures, it's for life."[24]

GOOD INFORMATION AND ADVICE

You will need the best current information and advice if you are to pursue a career successfully. This book may be filled with good advice, but it is not enough. You need to know the day-by-day developments in your medium.

The Trade Journals

Both the film and theatre worlds have trade journals that report current developments. In Hollywood, these are the *Hollywood Reporter* and *Daily Variety* for film and television, and *Drama-Logue* for theatre. The first two are published daily, and the latter weekly. In New York, *Show Business* and *Backstage*, both weeklies, cover all acting markets. The former publication regularly publishes lists of producers and agents; the latter one has an insert section with more extensive casting news and related developments. In addition, the New York weekly *Variety* provides worldwide coverage of all entertainment media. *Variety* is roughly four times the size of the others.

Not all of the trade papers are equally helpful to the beginning actor, or even to the veteran. The *Hollywood Reporter* and the two *Varieties* are addressed more to producers than to actors; if you subscribe to the *Hollywood Reporter*, for example, you will mainly be reading about who's producing what, and who's selling their Malibu mansion for two million six.

Drama-Logue, *Backstage*, and *Show Business*, however, are addressed directly to the actor and are filled with casting calls and advertisements that you will want to read. Naturally the casting calls are mainly for work that you can't get (auditions for which you must be submitted by an agent) or don't want ("erotic telegram services," nonpaying student films in New Jersey, cattle calls for shows already known to be cast, and so on), but there are always some legitimate opportunities, and even some illegitimate ones you're going to want to know about and investigate further.

Even beyond the casting calls, reading the trades gives you the feeling that you're part of the general goings-on. As such, they help you surmount the natural feeling of alienation and aloneness every newcomer feels when hitting New York or Hollywood for the first time. They *are* the news of show business, and a half hour with any one of them will give you a good vocabulary of names, places, and shows and an idea of what's in the heads of the agents, producers, and casting directors who are active at the moment. The trades give you, at the very least, a vicarious sense of participation, and even a vicarious participation is a good start in a business that considers itself a club. Indeed, reading the trades is part of your dues, whether you do it in a library, over someone's shoulder in the subway, or by sneaking into the members' lobby at Equity headquarters in New York.

Other Sources of Information

Where *else* do you get information? Talk to people. Actors love to talk about their business—some of them talk about almost nothing else. Acting schools are good places to begin, and theatre bars, particularly in New York (check out "Charley's" and "Joe Allen's" in the Broadway theatre district), are another. Or simply go to a lot of shows, such as the off-off Broadway workshops in New York or Los Angeles. Even if you don't know a soul in the production, hang around after the curtain call and wander backstage. If there were actors whose performances you liked, congratulate them (an always-effective calling card) and introduce yourself.

At worst, you will engage in an agreeable little conversation. At best, you will strike up a true and valuable friendship (some of the very best have begun in precisely this manner). And friends, of course, are a very fine source of information, perhaps the best there is. With friends in the trade you can get a feeling for the intangibles that control this emotional and frequently mystical business. You can sense out the tips, the hunches, the possibilities, and the probabilities that determine so much of the day-to-day course of the trade's events. You can get a sense of the feelings of the people in charge, and the people under them. Beware, naturally, of being overly influenced by any single person's likes, dislikes, neuroses, or phobias; be prepared to take comments with several grains of salt. Gradually you will gain a working knowledge of what casting possibilities are hot, which agents are really working for which actors, which producers are open to what kinds of suggestions, and in general what your competition is likely to be.

There are theatre schools that specialize in teaching you "how to audition" and "how to get a job," as well as "how to act." They may be useful. There are also actors' information services, actors' "rap groups," and actors' counseling services that are well-intentioned and often useful. You can find them, as well as public lectures on the actor's life, listed in the advertising sections of the trade papers. Of course, there are always a lot of people willing to take your money in return for "inside" tips and suggestions. With these people, you begin to reach the point of diminishing returns, however. No matter how much you may read or hear about the subject of "making it" in acting, nothing begins to approach the knowledge you get by working toward success yourself. The best way to learn the business is to get started, to participate. The suggestions in this book are designed to help you do that. Once you get your start, you can leave this book behind. You will find that you have access to information much more specifically applicable to your needs.

LUCK

Luck is placed last on this list simply because there is nothing you can do to get it. Luck is a factor that can outweigh most of the others, and there is nothing to do about it but groan. Shelly Duvall, a fine young film star, is a perfect example. At the time she was cast in the film *Brewster McCloud*, Duvall had never studied acting, had never seen a play, and generally disdained theatre people as "weird." She was a suburban housewife living in Houston, Texas and she was "discovered" while selling her husband's paintings to people who turned out to be MGM producers. The dream of "discovery" lies deep in the heart of every aspiring performer, but it comes almost as often to those who do not work for it as to those who do. Shirley MacLaine was "discovered" when she was called upon to substitute for Carol Haney in the Broadway musical, *Pajama Game*. Hal Wallis was in the audience, and but for this occurrence, Miss MacLaine might still be hoofing on 45th Street. It also turned out that MacLaine was planning to resign from the show the very night that Haney turned her ankle. But what do *you* do about luck? You don't go to Houston to sell oil paintings; that's for sure. You will have to find your own.

CHAPTER 3

THE FIRST DECISIONS

So, let's assume you have all these qualifications for an acting career that we've mentioned so far. Or you think you have them. You are going to look for work. What do you do now? First, you have to make some very important decisions.

YOUR GOAL

As with every course of action, you have to begin with a goal. That means two things: choosing a goal (that's the easy part), and *committing yourself* to achieving your goal.

In acting, your long-range career goal is simply to get cast. And cast *professionally*. In a play, a film, a television show, a repertory company, an industrial production, a TV commercial—something that will start off your career, get you into an acting union, and begin what you hope will be a long list of professional acting credits.

Who casts? In your high school, college, or community theatre, the director probably posted try-out notices on a bulletin board, or announced them in the local paper. You went to the appointed place, read from the script, and made it into the production. In the professional world, things are quite different.

Professional casting is done by many different people: the artistic directors of repertory theatres; the individual directors and producers of commercial plays, films, and TV shows; the producers of TV commercials and industrial productions; and, increasingly, by *casting directors* who now dominate film and television casting, and are making strong inroads into theatre casting as well. We refer to all of these as "casting people" in the following pages, and often several of them will have a voice in the casting of each role in a project.

Casting people, professionally, do not post try-out notices on a bulletin board, and they do not normally send out press releases on their auditions. Casting people are not easy to see; often they're not easy even to find. They do not keep open office hours, they do not usually answer their mail (not your mail, anyway), and they most certainly do not pick up their own telephones—at least not the telephones whose numbers you can obtain. They do not return your calls, and, indeed, when they do solicit overtures by mail, they specify, in capital letters and with exclamation points, ABSOLUTELY NO PHONE CALLS!!! How do you see such reclusive folks?

More important, how do you get them to see you? This is your basic problem. Creating the access between you, wanting to get cast, and the casting person who can make that happen, is the soul of acting professionally. Getting known, getting seen, getting accepted, getting cast, and getting work: This is the process you must negotiate.

First you must decide where to start. In which *medium.*

YOUR STARTING MEDIUM

The three main theatrical media are, of course, stage, film, and television. (There is also the possibility of starting out in comedy, nightclub work, or modeling, but you'll have to look elsewhere for guidance on these.)

These main media are divided into subgroups. Stage work can include Broadway and off-Broadway shows, stock and regional repertory companies, outdoor theatres, dinner theatres, industrial productions, and guest-artist stints at drama schools and universities. Film acting work largely consists of feature films, plus occasional short features and documentaries. Television can include filmed and taped TV specials, series episodes ("episodic TV" in the trade), movies of the week, series pilots, filmed or taped TV commercials, and live announcing positions. In which medium do you want to start your career? In which medium should you *try* to start your career? Where you will live and what you will do will be defined, in part at least, by your answer to that question.

You can simplify the question somewhat. From the acting point of view, film and TV are pretty much the same, since both involve acting for a camera (and usually a film camera, at that), and both are largely headquartered in Los Angeles. There is a status distinction and some long-term career considerations between the two, of course ("I want to be a performer when I'm 80 years old, and I think television can shorten your acting life very quickly," says Christopher Walken), but from a beginner's point of view you can explore both of them at the same time, and in the same town. The real question is: Stage work or camera work? Which one should you begin with?

You should first seek advice from your teachers and valued critic/ friends about the medium that best suits you. In weighing the alternatives open to you, you should take the following points into consideration.

Stage work demands great versatility and projection. Stage actors are called upon to do a wide variety of roles, frequently before a thousand or more people at one sitting. A strong, penetrating voice capable of great subtlety is an *absolute necessity*.

You should have a face that projects emotion without mugging, a body that moves well, and a personality that, without pushing, carries well beyond the footlights. Similarly, you should have a command of verse-speaking and classical acting styles, because most stage careers begin in theatres that produce classical plays. Strong talents in the areas of music and dance are increasingly valuable to the stage actor, though not absolutely necessary.

Above all, the stage actor needs the great intangibles: talent, presence, and timing. You must be able to enunciate the subtlest nuances clearly to huge audiences without looking as if you are reading from a speech textbook, and you must convey the sense of a vibrant personality whether you are playing romantic lead, villain, or village idiot.

If your talents lie, on the other hand, in the area of extremely naturalistic performing, a film or television job will probably be more suitable for a start. Acting before a camera ruthlessly shows up all but the most honest of performers. It virtually eliminates the need for projection, since the microphone can be placed just inches away. It has been said that the film actor is the pawn of the film's technicians: "The cameraman usurps the actor's physical composition, the sound mixer his intonation, and the editor his timing." Thus, for the camera actor it is personality, looks, honesty, and the ineffable "quality" that become premium ingredients.

In general, a person's looks count less in live theatre than in film or TV, mainly because makeup can do much more at fifty feet than in a larger-than-life close-up. Many people who are genuinely plain have had brilliant stage careers but have found it impossible to get work in

Hollywood. By contrast, a person who is astonishingly beautiful, or interesting in a unique way, can get film or TV work almost on that basis alone.

Can you choose *both* media? Of course you can, eventually. Actors jump media with great frequency these days, and television performers are now almost as common on Broadway as stage actors are on the big and small screens. But you're not going to start in two media simultaneously, even if you plan to be eventually active in all of them. A journey of a thousand miles begins with a single step, Confucius said. You're going to begin with *one* part in *one* medium, and you should put all your focus into that one—for a start.

CHOOSING A HOME BASE

Where will you live?   As an actor you really have only three choices: New York, Los Angeles-Hollywood, or the spiderweb of regional circuits. These choices involve different kinds of theatrical activity and different life-styles and business procedures for you.

The big cities are, of course, New York and L.A., and "bi-coastal" actors now share their time between the Big Apple, home of Broadway, off-Broadway, and most of TV's soap operas and commercials; and the Big Orange, production home of the seven major film studios, most TV producers, and hundreds of professional and quasi-professional stage showcases each year. But before turning to the "big bigs," let's look around the rest of the country first.

REGIONAL THEATRE: THE LORT– STOCK–DINNER CIRCUIT

Regional theatre is very likely where you will start out, and perhaps should start out. First, it probably exists close to home, and/or close to your college or university; you may already attend a few on a regular basis. Second, it's a far more *accessible* professional environment than New York or Los Angeles, and you can contact the artistic staff fairly directly. Regional theatre, unlike the "big bigs," is relatively free from the machinations of agents, managers, associate producers, or other middlemen. Not only is it a good place to start out— many actors find it an equally good place to "end up."

Regional theatre is a general term, and not entirely specific. Generally, one uses it to include the spectrum of nonprofit theatre companies, sometimes called "resident companies," throughout the country (including the nonprofit theatre companies in New York City) plus commercial dinner theatres and stock companies out of New York.

The nonprofit (or "not-for-profit") sector is of the greatest current importance, and has experienced a meteoric growth in the past generation. It now includes close to 300 theatres, all of professional status, that are loosely linked as constituents of the Theatre Communications Group (TCG). TCG was founded in 1961, beginning the regional theatre "movement," at a time when there were only sixteen regional theatre companies in the country. TCG has doubled and redoubled many times since, until virtually every city of importance in the United States has at least one nonprofit theatre presenting productions and hiring actors. Regional theatre is no longer a "movement"; it is, quite simply, the major segment of American theatre. TCG offices are (where else?) in New York City, at 355 Lexington Avenue (New York, NY 10017); the office provides a number of publications on regional theatre and its 300-odd constituent companies.

Virtually *all* of these TCG constituent theatres audition new actors from time to time. Each constituent company is listed and described in the regular TCG publication, *Theatre Profiles*, which is revised every two or three years. The 1988 edition (*Theatre Profiles 8*) describes 211 constituent companies, with key staff names, addresses, phone numbers, production photos, company ideologies, and sample seasons.

All nonprofit professional theatres are categorized by the Equity contracts under which they operate. Those theatres linked into the League of Resident Theatres (LORT), and operating under the LORT contracts (there are five categories of contract—A, B+, B, C, and D—depending on the theatre's size), are the cream of the nonprofit crop.

LORT is an association of more than eighty first-class nonprofit professional theatres in the major American cities. You've heard of many of them: the Arena Stage in Washington, D.C., the Guthrie Theatre in Minneapolis, the American Conservatory Theatre in San Francisco, the Long Wharf Theatre in New Haven, the South Coast Repertory Theatre in Costa Mesa, the Seattle Repertory Theatre. LORT theatres ordinarily produce independent work of exceptionally high quality; virtually all the Tony and Pulitzer Prize-winning American plays of the 1980s were first mounted by LORT companies. Since 1985, LORT has also provided the bulk of professional stage acting jobs, counting 63,123 actor work weeks in 1988, which is more than Broadway (27,118) and Broadway road shows (20,328) combined.

LORT's association with TCG has given the theatres a national "network" and an international identity, much of which is promoted by their in-house (but widely distributed) monthly magazine, *American Theater*, which lists current schedules around the country. Many of the LORT theatres have federal grants to pursue experimental work and talent development; some have affiliations with universities, and others have conservatories of their own. In addition to their stage work, many LORT theatres have been invited to have their productions taped for national Public Broadcasting System (PBS) telecasting, and this trend will surely grow as PBS develops tie-ins with pay TV and national "cultural network" subscription services. Clearly, for an actor, the LORT circuit is the plum of regional theatre activities. The best work of these theatres, while appealing primarily to their local audience, is regularly reviewed in trade papers, scholarly journals, and occasionally in *Newsweek, Time,* and the *New York Times.* An annual Tony Award gives further national prominence to the most outstanding LORT companies.

Other nonprofit theatres in the TCG circuit also offer regular employment for actors, and sometimes even better break-in opportunities for acting aspirants. CATs (Chicago Area Theatres) are smaller-than-LORT (but still professional) companies in the Chicago area, including the superlative Steppenwolf Company. Equity also maintains a BAT for the (San Francisco) Bay Area non-LORT companies—including San Francisco's Magic and Eureka Theatres, the Oakland Ensemble Theatre, and the San Jose Stage Company—that produce in the nine Bay area counties. The BAT contract also includes a BAPP (for Bay Area Project Policy) waiver—permitting professional actors to work without a union contract for certain small Bay Area shows.

The SPT (Small Professional Theater) contract was initiated by Equity in 1985. It is an agreement whereby theatres too small for LORT membership can still employ professionals, together with an equal number (or less) of local amateurs. SPT theatres reported 16,710 work weeks in 1987-1988, about one-quarter of the LORT total. Some forty to sixty theatres are STPs, mostly companies that plan to become LORT in a few years. Examples in 1989 included the Detroit Repertory Theatre, the Washington (D.C.) Stage Guild, the Portland (Maine) Repertory Theatre, and the Boars Head: Michigan Public Theatre.

Still more professional actor work weeks in the regional theatre come about through individual LOA (Letter of Agreement) contracts, Guest Artist/Actor-Teacher contracts, Special contracts, Mini contracts, Theatre for Young Audience contracts, and University/Resident Theater contracts. All these contracts cover professional actors who work with a variety of loosely formed companies, or with collegiate or other academic groups.

And there are many regional theatres that are *not* part of TCG, and that are also *not* nonprofit—companies that are privately owned. These are largely stock companies (including summer stock) and dinner theatres. There are also stock packaging companies that tour summer productions, and certain city-based musical theatre producing groups.

Stock companies, organized under the Equity CORST or COST contracts, (CORST = Council of Resident Stock Theatres; COST = Council of Stock Theatres) present plays for stock runs, usually one or more weeks, and usually in the summer only, although some go year-round. CORST theatres must have a resident company of at least seven Equity members; many CORST theatres have apprentice programs and offer some possibilities for local actors (called "local jobbers") as well. COST theatres need have no stable company, and in fact frequently produce prepackaged shows that simply bus from one COST theatre to another each week. Weekly stock—particularly at the New England summer theatres that once formed a "straw hat circuit"—used to be the great break-in venue for acting aspirants. This is where Mickey Rooney and Judy Garland found an old barn and said "Hey, let's put on a play." But summer stock has now been relatively eclipsed, as a professional starting place, by the more intense LORT and even SPT resident movements.

Dinner theatres, which burst upon the American theatre scene in the early 1970s, have fallen back somewhat since then, but have now stabilized in numbers, in the 1980s, at about one-third of the mid-70s high. A national association (the American Dinner Theatre Association) links most Equity companies, and a National Dinner Theatre Association links most non-Equity ones—the latter group holds regional unified auditions, too. Dinner theatres provide another 21,000 professional actor work weeks on the dinner theatre contract. The theatrical fare consists, in the main, of light comedies and musicals; the plays are combined not only with pretheatre dinners, but occasionally posttheatre dancing and merriment, comprising a fairly encompassing entertainment medium. Some dinner theatres are beginning to offer apprentice programs, and apprentices who elect to serve as waiters and waitresses can make up to $400 per week while training. Occasionally dinner theatres offer year-round employment, which is a godsend to most actors; conversely the dinner theatre credit is not always a particularly helpful stepping stone to "eatless" ventures.

And there are some non-Equity companies—some employing Equity Guest Artists—in the regions too, which form sort of a fringe to the professional theatre. Shakespeare Festivals, featuring the Bard of Avon, and Outdoor Drama Festivals, featuring pageants of American history, are major groups of summer theatre companies, offering a range from well-paying to low-paying to no-paying opportunities in many states around the country. There are literally dozens of Shakespeare Festivals, including important ones in Oregon, Utah, Colorado, Texas, New Jersey, Vermont, Connecticut, California, Alabama, New York, Illinois, Idaho, among others. Most have at least some professional actors in key roles, but all audition nonprofessionals, at least for smaller parts. Summer theatre directories, such as that published by Jill Charles, lists addresses and the audition dates for most of them. Many of the non-Shakespearean outdoor theatres are associated in an Institute of Outdoor Drama, headquartered at the University of North Carolina (see the appendix), which conducts annual unified auditions for many of its members.

The regional theatre offers a certain amount of work, a *direct* opportunity to break into the field (in that you can apply to audition directly for many of these theatres, not via the auspices of an agent), and the occasional possibility of intermediate engagements via apprenticeships and journeyman contracts—something that does not occur in New York or Los Angeles.

You can work your way up to a union (Equity) card in many regional theatres, once you're on board. Fifty weeks of acting work with some of them, even at a combination of some of them, can qualify you for membership in the Actors' Equity Association, if the theatre participates in the union's "Equity Membership Candidate Program." LORT, most Equity stock and dinner companies, and some SPT, CAT, and LOA companies participate. This provision clearly indicates the value of a year's work, even as an understudy or unpaid spear carrier, at a professional regional theatre working under Equity agreements. You can also earn your *Eligible Performer card* at some regional theatres—if, in four consecutive weeks of acting there, you earn a sum equal to or more than the lowest current Equity minimum salary. There's a full discussion of the Equity Membership Candidate Program, and the Eligible Performer card, in the "Unions" section of this chapter.

Overall, the regional theatre (both profit and nonprofit) has become America's primary break-in place for actors, and it remains a significant employment area for American stage actors, even for Broadway veterans. Films and television also draw from regional banks. Casting director Mike Fenton reports that regional theatre is the source of 60% of the "unknowns" in Hollywood.[25] And the number of regional plays that make their way to New York, with the same casts, is growing rapidly. Such Steppenwolf regulars as John Malkovich, Joan Allen, Glenne Headly, and Gary Sinise have developed wonderful national reputations from their Chicago-based works.

But you must not assume that there is an automatic communication network among these theatres. Regional theatre remains in the regions, and credits there, however respectable, do not automatically turn into stepping stones to Broadway or Hollywood—if that's where you think you're headed. Regional credits may not even serve as stepping stones to other regional theatres, and actors employed at some of America's more remote companies, such as the Oregon Shakespeare Festival at Ashland, often find it difficult to audition for future jobs elsewhere while toiling away in the shadow of the Siskiyou Mountains. At Ashland and similar theatres, actors have created "shares" programs, at their own expense, flying in various LORT artistic directors to audition company members for future work at other theatres. To work in the regional theatre ("the provinces," they would say in England) is to develop a primarily local reputation, not a national one, and if you then plan to head for New York or Los Angeles, you had still better plan to start at the bottom when you get there (albeit with some valuable credentials).

Some actors, of course, have no wish to "go Hollywood" or to head for the Great White Way in the East. Hundreds of actors all over the country delightedly spend their entire careers in regional theatre, finding there a high degree of artistic fulfillment *and* social satisfaction. The Tony Award-winning South Coast Repertory Company in Costa Mesa (California) has maintained a core professional acting company (Don Took, Ron Boussom, Martha McFarland, Art Koustic, Hal Landon) for twenty-five years, thus proving that regular (if perhaps unspectacular) acting employment *does* still exist in the American theatre. But most actors eventually get frustrated after a decade or so in the regional circuits. Rene Auberjonois, a superb regional actor who "went on" to Broadway and Hollywood success, gives these reasons for leaving LORT: "Most actors in regional theatre are schizophrenics; they cannot reconcile the feeling that they should be fighting the fight of commercial theatre with the feeling that they are chosen members of some great and holy theatrical crusade. This dilemma gives rise to a working climate which could be compared to a monastery filled with self-consciously zealous monks suppressing the desire to ravage the neighboring village."[26] It is evident that some of this "schizophrenia" is felt, if not to the same degree, by many in the LORT-CORST-COST circuit.

Getting Into Regional Theatres

You may audition for regional theatres locally (at the theatre itself), in New York, or at certain centralized regional locations. A discussion of these possibilities follows. You should treat the opportunity to audition as a privilege, not a right. It is never automatic, the way it is in most colleges and universities, and, in fact, you may be turned down cold for an audition more often than not. But it's a lot easier than auditioning for a Broadway show or a Hollywood film: You *can* get a hearing if you are qualified—and persistent.

In almost all cases, it will help if you are certified as an *Eligible Performer*. This is a formal Actors' Equity Association designation that you have to apply for; in 1988 it replaced (for audition purposes) the distinction between Equity and non-Equity performers. The EP designation, which permits you to attend open calls, can be achieved if you have worked for four weeks as a salaried actor (even in a nonunion theatre), or for forty weeks as an apprentice in an Equity company. There's quite a bit more to it than that, though; read the fuller discussion in the section called "Unions," later in this chapter.

Auditioning Locally

Much regional casting is now done right at home. Most LORT, and virtually all SPT, LOA, and dinner companies cast, at least in part, on their own premises. Some local casting calls, to be sure, are merely public relations charades, intended to give the community a sense of participation, and to generate for the theatre company local good will—as well as donors and subscribers. But the growth of strong academic drama programs across the nation, and the proliferation of the regional theatres themselves, has created a national talent pool— a talent pool in every big city in the country—that regional theatres (as well as film companies looking for extras "on location") draw upon more and more regularly.

Ordinarily, local casting begins by way of "generals," or "general auditions," rather than by specific role auditions. You can come to a theatre company's attention through a general, and can be brought in for specific auditions when the opportunity presents itself. This means hanging around the area for some time, of course, or being able to drop in on short notice.

Actors in general are asked to perform one or two monologues; if two, these would ordinarily be requested in contrasting styles. Generals can be held on a regular, recurring schedule. The Mark Taper Forum in Los Angeles, for example, sees noneligible L.A. performers on a drop-in basis between 10:00 A.M. and 12:00 noon on the first Monday of each month. Eligible performers can call on that same day for an appointment, which will be honored later. (*Note*: Don't act on this, or other casting information, without double-checking the theatre's current policy!) Other theatres hold bimonthly or semiannual or annual auditions. One LORT artistic director writes, quite typically:

> Locally, we see anyone who wants to come to audition, eligible or ineligible. We hold open calls once in the fall (which is the best time, because we're really looking for actors then), and once in the spring (not such a good time, because we're thinking more of relieving the congestion in the "waiting line" than casting our winter season). We ask each person to prepare (memorize) two contrasting selections of about two minutes each, and to send in or bring with them an 8 x 10 and a resume.

Nonprofit New York theatres also hold general auditions, limited to eligible performers only. The New York Shakespeare Festival, for example, holds ten days of generals spaced throughout the year. These auditions are always announced in the New York trade papers, *Back Stage* and *Show Business*. A monologue of up to five minutes is required. Most New York City companies use the Actors' Equity Association Audition Center for sign-ups and for determining eligibility.

Letters of inquiry, or telephone calls, to theatres in your area will get you information about the time and place of general auditions you qualify for. The same is true for dinner theatres; write them and ask! The Executive Secretary of the American Dinner Theatre Institute writes:

> The only effective method of securing employment in dinner theatres currently is to write to each theatre in which you are interested and request an audition. From my experience, if a young actor is willing to make the trip, he will be given a courteous reception and an unhurried audition.

These are not promises, but probabilities.

So write or call any theatre that strikes your fancy, and that you are willing to travel to (and remain in the area of), and try to arrange for an appointment, or an open-call audition. Be prepared with at least two photos and resumes (one to send ahead, one to have ready to give them if they've mislaid the first) and be prepared to write again—and again—if your original letter goes unanswered. Most LORT theatres receive between 400 and 1,000 new resumes and applications *per week* during their casting seasons, and few of these companies have the facilities and staff to process this enormous correspondence with complete accuracy. Make the most out of any reply you get.

As to your chances of gaining employment as an ineligible performer with a LORT company, they are small but not absolutely zero. Sometimes you will be just right for a role, and they will snap you up. Some theatres maintain small non-Equity (non-EP) companies: the Pennsylvania Stage Company, for example, engages a group of "Acting Associates" for smaller parts in their season. The Berkeley Repertory Theatre has a second company that does walk-ons, understudies principal roles, and mounts touring productions. They are paid $175 a week and get their Equity cards in two years. Many other opportunities for non-Equity and ineligible actors at LORT companies occur at the B, C, and D levels, where Equity rules permit a freer use of nonunion performers. Keith Fowler, former artistic director at the Virginia Museum (LORT C) Theatre (now Theatre Virginia), expressed that company's philosophy as follows:

> The best chance an ineligible performer has for getting a role from us is to be, first of all, an outstanding actor, and secondly a local resident. Then we know he will be easily available and won't need much money to live on. The odds against the auditioning actor are, of course, incredibly high. We see a good many fine actors, both eligible and noneligible. We have a very good selection to choose from; it's a buyers' market. What isn't widely known is that we often see fresh faces that we want very much to give jobs to. I can think of three actors right now that I would dearly love to work with. Sometimes the roles aren't right for these people though, and you can't use them, much as you'd like to. More often, you can think of roles, but you already have actors who are just as good and who are already your friends and artistic companions, and you're certainly not going to bump them out of their jobs to make room for the new face. We have to remember that auditioning is a process for discovering a few new actors for your company, not casting all

> your roles. Most roles are cast with actors who are already
> hardworking members of your ensemble.

So understand the picture, and try to fit yourself into it one way or another.

Auditioning in New York

Many LORT and developing theatres audition in New York City, both for general and specific calls. These are not easy to get into, but you can try.

The LORT Lottery   LORT schedules two New York auditions each year, selecting auditionees—from among eligible performers only—by *lottery*. December and May are the audition months, with three days of each month given to the purpose. Eligible performers must submit their application for the audition lottery well in advance. It should be on a 3 x 5 card with your name, address, phone number, Social Security number, and Eligible Performer Audition Card Number. Registration in person is urged, although not absolutely required, and if you are selected to audition (the list of lottery winners is posted in the Equity office) you must confirm in person, unless you live more than 100 miles away. There are many more specific regulations regarding the LORT lottery, which you should check out at the time from the New York AEA office (165 West 46th Street, New York 10036), or by reading the trades well in advance of the appropriate dates. A three-minute audition is what you get for your trouble.

Many LORT and developing theatres also cast independently in New York, usually at the AEA Audition Center, but sometimes at rented studios elsewhere in the city. You will be given preference as an eligible performer, but if there's time, ineligible performers may also be seen.

Regional Combined Auditions

Wouldn't it be wonderful to go to one single audition, and be seen by hundreds of artistic directors from around the country? This happens in other countries. Graduates of the Finnish National Theatre School, for example, audition in Helsinki at the end of their course of instruction for all the stage directors in Finland, and at the end of the audition, every graduate has a job! (On the other hand, only one in several hundred applicants make it into the Theatre School.) The diversification of theatre in this country, and the proliferation of drama schools, have made such cross-country auditions impossible, although for years TCG did run such a national audition, as did the now-defunct League of Professional Theatre Training Schools. TCG dropped their national audition in 1981, owing to "the growing tendency of theatres to cast show-by-show rather than full seasons, the relatively few theatres offering continuing employment to graduating students, and the increasing tendency of theatres to cast regionally rather than centrally," according to TCG executives.

There are several major groups that continue to hold unified regional auditions, however, and these are of varying use to the actor seeking employment.

The University/Resident Theatre Association (U/RTA) holds auditions at selected locales throughout the United States for nominated college students, followed by three finalist auditions in the New York, Chicago, and Los Angeles areas. These are not, ordinarily, auditions for professional work, however. Most of the opportunities offered by U/RTA are for paid graduate assistantships and fellowships at university drama programs, some of which are associated with resident theatres. Therefore, most of the U/RTA offerings will involve your enrollment in a Ph.D. or M.F.A. program at the host campus. Still, you may simultaneously or subsequently become involved with a related professional theatre company, and the U/RTA has proven to be a useful, if indirect, route to professional employment. For this reason, U/RTA should be investigated by interested college seniors. Write directly to U/RTA headquarters (1540 Broadway, Suite 3704, New York, NY 10036) for details and try to get a nomination from your drama department chairperson.

Several other unified auditions, listed below, are for a mix of summer theatres, special summer productions, and some year-round companies. If you're interested, you should write for applications to these auditioning groups in December or January, to get a March or April audition for a summer acting job. Always include a business-sized self-addressed stamped envelope (SASE) with your request, and be prepared to pay a small auditioning fee. Remember, audition spaces are limited, and you may not even make it in; apply early, and present the strongest possible application. The main regional auditioners (as of 1989):

The *Institute of Outdoor Drama*, 3240 Graham Memorial, University of North Carolina, Chapel Hill, NC 27599-3240.   This is an association of historical pageants, performed (obviously) out-doors. The pay is often quite good. The IOD will see 200 preregistered applicants, who must be at least 18 and have theatrical training. If you get in, you will be seen by about sixteen theatre companies from seven states, including (in 1989) *The Lost Colony* at Manteo, NC; *Young Abe Lincoln* at Lincoln City, Indiana; and *Tecumseh!* in Chillicothe, Ohio.

The *Southeastern Theatre Conference* (SETC) is also headquartered at a University of North Carolina campus; SETC's annual con-vention includes a group audition for about eighty theatre companies, both summer and year-round. Send your SASE to the SETC at 311 McIver Street, University of North Carolina at Greensboro, Greensboro, NC 27412. You will have to join the SETC to audition, but you can do that at the convention itself, and then participate in the other convention activities. Some of the 1989 participants were the Heritage Repertory Theatre of Charlottesville, Virginia; the Great American People Show in Champaign, Illinois; and the Sweet Fanny Adams Theatre & Music Hall of Gatlinburg, Tennessee. There is a fee for audi-tioning, which includes your SETC membership and convention fee.

New England Theatre Conference, 50 Exchange Street, Waltham, MA 02154. The NETC sees about 700 actors for nearly sixty theatre companies. Your application will be screened first (only about half the applicants are admitted to the audition), and there is a small audition fee. Certain LORT internship pro-grams also audition here as well; among the many companies attending in 1988 were the Dorset Theatre Festival, the Cape Cod Melody Tent, the Boothbay Dinner Theatre, the Shawney Playhouse, the Virginia Stage Company, the Berkshire Play-house, the Actor's Theatre of Louisville, and the Nutmeg Summer Theatre, among others.

Strawhat Auditions take place in New York City; send for infor-mation to StrawHat, Box 382-A, Planetarium Station, New York, NY 10024. Your completed application must include a photo-resume, which will be reprinted and distributed to the produc-ers at the auditions. About thirty companies participate, mostly from upstate New York. There is a fee.

Midwest Theatre Auditions, Conservatory of Theatre Arts, Webster University, 470 E. Lockwood, St. Louis, MO 63119. About sixty companies are involved here.

Ohio Theatre Alliance, 504 N. Park Street, Columbus, OH 43215. About thirty companies.

Many other states and areas have theatre associations that conduct regional auditions, often at a different location every year. You can find out more by contacting your state or regional theatre association.

Regional Concentrations

Well, if there is an "increasing tendency of theatres to cast regionally"—and there is—then it makes sense to try establishing yourself in one of those regions in which there is a real concentration of LORT and developing (SPT and LOA) theatres. These are the areas around Chicago, Los Angeles, Seattle, San Diego, Washington, Philadelphia, and San Francisco—somewhat in that order. If you live in one of these towns, or have a place to stay for a few months in any of these areas, you can first test the professional waters. Any one of these places would make a good place to start. You should write ahead for interviews and auditions, but the real action won't take place until you arrive. Apart from general auditions, you can visit the casting offices, contact the directors and stage managers, and apply for nonacting positions that would put you in the artistic director's line of sight. Ask about their new-play-reading series, or suggest they set one up. Get to know the people involved, *see the productions*, write a play yourself and submit it, get on the team any way you can. You may, of course, have to work your way in through the back door, but that's as good a way as any to gain a foothold in the business. Remember, every theatre has opportunities opening, often unexpectedly, all the time. Frequently, "break-in" situations come about at the last minute: a role is written into a new play that opens next week, and there's a new intern who is just right for it. Bingo. Resident companies, while professional, are not as rigidly unionized as Broadway productions or Hollywood films, and "being in the family" can become more important than "being in the union" in a crisis situation.

THE BIG TOWNS

Sooner or later, of course, you're at least going to think about going to New York or Los Angeles. These are the "big bigs," as we've said (and as you know), and there aren't too many people who go into this business who don't harbor some ambition to measure their powers in the most celebrated theatrical arenas: New York and Los Angeles. But which one?

How to Choose?

Which town is easiest to "break into"? Neither, of course, is remotely easy, and there is no simple answer to the question; there are hundreds of variable factors. Most actors eventually try them both. Beware of those who say that "New York is finished" or "L.A. is impossible." Both these cities are tough, of course, but both will be employing hundreds of new actors each year; *each* one is finished for some, impossible for others.

Of course, you should know something about the towns themselves. They are utterly unalike, and both take some getting used to. New York is riddled with urban blight, nowhere more than in the theatre districts. Homeless folks camp out right under the theatre marquees; the *New York Times* has taken to calling the town "New Calcutta." Rents in the city are unbelievably high, for unbelievably shabby apartments—and middling restaurants charge twice what they do in Cleveland or Spokane. Substance abuse is a sidewalk sport in this town, and crime is endemic. On the other hand—well, this is America's premiere city, and for most of us New York's problems are dwarfed by its sheer magnificence. It's our publishing, broadcasting, advertising, art, and finance capital, as well as our theatre capital, and even a marginal life in New York City provides a heady climate and a thrilling intensity for any committed theatre artist. It's shocking how many plays are *set* here. New York, for all its flagrant faults, is at the very pulse of American culture, and not to know New York is to remain apart, to some extent, from the soul of the American stage.

Los Angeles, by contrast, is barely a city at all, but rather a vast desert plain, alternately broken up by urban concentrations (Hollywood, "downtown," Century City, Beverly Hills, Westwood, Universal City) and residential pastures—all crisscrossed by freeways to nowhere and the world's most indifferent system of public transportation. There is little in the way of an "L.A. Scene," since the city is vastly spread out and decentralized, and the people are among the most privacy conscious on earth. The real action of L.A. takes place within private homes and gated studios, and over Pacific Bell telephones—most of which (it often seems) are located in automobiles. The cellular conversation between two cars on the freeway is L.A.'s classic connection.

But geography is probably not the crucial factor in this decision. The key question is: Which acting *medium* do you plan to act in, or at least to begin your career in?

Well-trained stage actors, classical actors, and musical theatre performers should *usually* head for New York, for that's where most professional stage shows and musicals are cast—virtually all on- and off-Broadway; most stock (COST and CORST) and dinner; much LORT, SPT, and LOA. Even top-flight L.A. theatres cast a good deal in New York, infuriating southern California stage actors no end.

Conversely, those whose primary focus is on film and television work—particularly actors whose on-camera looks and personalities, and naturalistic acting abilities, are more likely to be selling points than stage training and experience—should head for Hollywood, the land of TV studios and feature films, as well as countless ninety-nine-seat showcase theatres, where actors perform on stage so as to be cast in films.

So, if you're bigger than life, musical or rep-oriented, and eminently stageworthy, head for the Big Apple. And if you're drop-dead gorgeous, personality plus, intimate and contemporary, head instead for the Big Orange.

But, naturally, most actors fall somewhere in between. Wouldn't it be wonderful to live in England, where classical theatre, commercial theatre, films, and television are all headquartered in the same city? Where should the American in-betweens go? On margin (and this is a difficult call), this author recommends New York: first, because it is easier to get seen there; second, because there's more you can do there without an agent; third, because you won't need a car; fourth, because minor New York stage credits are more important in Hollywood these days than minor Hollywood TV credits are in New York; and fifth, because New York is the central casting locus for the regional theatre circuit. New York is also the home of the soap opera, a break-in ground of increasing importance, and the site of most commercial shoots, cruise ship bookings, and business theatre (musical extravaganzas produced by corporations for their employees or stockholders), which are all good sources of revenue. So if you think you're going to want to try both towns, I'd say: Try New York first.

Some of the best film actors today began their careers in the live theatre of the regions and in New York: Sigourney Weaver, Stacy

Keach, Robert Duvall, Daniel Travanti, Al Pacino, Frank Langella, Meryl Streep, Barbra Streisand, Jane Alexander, Robert DeNiro, Robert Redford, Dustin Hoffman, and Richard Dreyfuss, for example. Stage to film, and New York to L.A., is the classic route. As the late James Coco said, "Off-Broadway auditions for Broadway, which auditions for Hollywood." More than ever before, film and even television directors look for actors well versed in improvisation, in stage acting—yes, even in classical performance technique. There are, of course, many Hollywood directors who shy away from what they feel are "arty off-Broadway know-it-alls." But New York credits are an important plus in any L.A. actor's portfolio. So if you're undecided between the two, and aiming to make your first career moves in stage acting (although it might not necessarily work out that way), New York should be your destination.

If, on the other hand, you are charismatic only on camera, are extraordinarily beautiful, or are determined to be a film or television performer, we'll say it again: Go west.

CHAPTER 4

ESTABLISHING YOURSELF

You have moved, then, to your new city. The first thing you must do is to *establish* yourself. Obviously you need a place to stay, and rents in both New York and L.A. are quite expensive—New York extraordinarily so (not to mention the rental agency, or "fixture," commissions you will probably be hit up for as well.) If possible, move in with a friend and give yourself a couple of weeks to look for a rent-stabilized apartment in a decent area; better yet, move to New York with a friend or two and share a place and the rent among you. Bring enough money to pay two months' rent in advance plus a deposit, plus a thousand dollars in reserve. (Why a thousand dollars? It's a good round sum, and you'll need some real breathing room. Any less and you'll be in a state of constant fiscal panic before the end of the first week. But if it's out of the question, well, go anyway.)

If you head for Los Angeles, you can expect to find a more reasonably priced place to stay. It will also be cleaner and nicer to come home to. The limitation of L.A. is that you absolutely must have a *car* in good running condition. This will eat up whatever you may save on rent. (A car is not only unnecessary in New York, the parking rates there will make it a real liability, so leave your Toyota in Toledo.)

Once you are settled, you can get to work. There will be many things you need. There is no particular order in which you should get them, but you should get them fast. These are:

- A dependable source of income
- A telephone and a telephone service
- Photos

- A resume of your training and experience
- Colleagues
- Up-to-date information

A DEPENDABLE SOURCE OF INCOME

Obviously you need a source of income that you can count on. You can't pay your bills, eat, dress, or go out into the world without money. Moreover, you cannot afford to scrimp on professional expenses like photographs and classes. Perhaps you have regular income from home, or from your working (and indulgent) spouse, or from a friend. If so, you need not worry as long as your source continues to take care of you, though generally something is expected in return. If you aren't so lucky, you will have to get a job, and preferably one with flexible hours that pays well. In Hollywood, since most work and interviews take place in the daytime, an evening job is ideal. For this reason, most L.A. area waiters are unemployed actors: Table waiting is *the* job of choice for most Hollywood thesps. In New York the same is true, until you start to perform or work at night in off-off-Broadway, when a morning or grave-yard shift may be preferable. The back pages of *Backstage* and other trades advertise openings for temporary secretaries, word processors, administrative assistants, guy/gal Fridays, receptionists, bilinguals, clerks, and typists: If you have office skills, you can make a living in either town.

A salable office skill is particularly valuable—you might land a job in a theatre-related area, and you will start to get contacts while you work. Many young men and women (male secretaries are now commonplace in Hollywood and are becoming so in New York) have started in the office, and ended up on stage. If you can, do something you can be proud of, something you feel is professional. Being a professional at something is good training for being a professional at acting. Stay away from porn movies and illicit activities that may beckon; they will make you feel bad about yourself, which isn't going to help your acting one bit.

A TELEPHONE AND TELEPHONE ANSWERING SERVICE

You cannot do anything in show business without both a telephone and a telephone service or answering machine. You must be reachable to get work, and absolutely nobody in New York or Los Angeles relies on the mails for this. A telephone is simply an essential, and you should order yours with the "call waiting" feature, which will let the producer's call come through with the job offer even when you're talking to your mother. You can expect to make some toll and long-distance calls, too; your professional telephone bill might run $40 a month without anything terribly special showing on it.

Of course, you're not going to wait at home for the phone to ring, so you also need a telephone service or telephone answering machine. The best services (about $50 per month) will pick up on calls made to your number when you're out (via an electronic hookup); cheaper services (about $10) will take messages for you at their own number (which you list as your "service number.") They can then forward your calls or call you (at an extra charge), or beep your beeper if you carry one (at an *extra* extra charge), or they will hold messages until you call in for them—which you should do two or three times a day. Learn to live with the bright voice on the other end who gaily declares, "No messages today!" or "All clear!"

You can also get an answering machine; most actors do, even when they have a service number as well. You probably know these devices; they hook up to your phone, play your message, and receive messages "after the tone." You can even call some of them from another phone to hear your messages. The problem with answering machines, which are cheaper than services in the long run, is that a lot of casting people won't bother giving a message to a tape recorder—they'll just call someone else. It's harder to hang up on a human service operator, and if the service operator forwards the call, you can be reached much more of the time.

Want to go all the way? Get a cellular phone for your car. No need to miss one casting call just because you're driving to another! But this might have to wait for your first starring role—it's expensive.

PHOTOGRAPHS

Your photos are your calling cards; no actor can be without them. You may want them in three basic forms:

- Photos for distribution. These are mass-produced head shots, and, together with your resume, are given out to anybody who seems to have a professional reason for wanting them.

These are your *most important photos*, but you may also want:

- Composites, which combine a variety of head shots and other photos. Composites are used more often for commercials than for regular acting roles.

- Photos for your "book," which you may carry around to interviews and auditions, and show to interested directors and producers. The "book" is seen more rarely these days, however, and, like the composite, is important mainly for model and commercial casting.

You can acquire photos for all these purposes at the same time. The standard procedure is to go to a photographer and have a sitting. You will then get a set of contact prints (usually seventy-two or more, if the sitting is with a 35-millimeter camera, which most are) from which you can select a few shots (perhaps a dozen) to be enlarged to full size (8" x 10"). You can then select one or two head shots to have mass-duplicated, and the others will go in your book.

The photographer might charge as little as $100, or as much as the traffic will bear: $250 to $400 is a medium range for well-respected New York and Hollywood photographers that know the acting field, and four-figure fees are not unusual. The price usually includes at least one or two enlargements; maybe more.

You don't get your mass-produced copies from the photographer, but from a reproduction service, which will charge you $40 or so per hundred 8 x 10s. You can have your name printed on the margin of each photo for a little extra. You can also have photo-postcards printed, with your head shot on one side, and a place for an address, message, and stamp on the other. This will be used to confirm dates, invite agents to your shows, and keep your picture before the casting people.

It's easy to find photographers and photo reproduction services. There are dozens of advertisements for each in *Back Stage*, *Show Business*, and *Drama-Logue*. Finding *good* photographers is a little more difficult, and a lot more subjective.

Everyone has an idea about what a good photograph should be, and almost everybody will tell you that *your* photos are horrible. They probably *are* horrible, if they were made by your amateur boyfriend, or at your home town portrait studio. What actually constitutes a good actor photo, however, is a highly subjective subject, particularly when *you're* the subject. Try to be as objective as you can, and hear all opinions with a grain of salt; remember, you are looking for a photo that will get you work, not please your mother.

Your basic "calling-card" photo should be an engaging 8 x 10 black and white head shot, professionally produced, and it should *look like you*. It should also look natural and alive. It should be *appealing*— people should *like* looking at it. And it should be distinctive—people should *remember* it.

Before looking at photographers, look at some photographs. Check out the *Players Directory* at the Academy of Motion Picture Arts and Sciences office (8949 Wilshire Boulevard, Beverly Hills; there's a room for studying them on the eighth floor), or the *Players Guide* in an agent's lobby in New York. These two books are where most professional actors, stars and unknowns, have their current head shots on view for prospective producers and casting directors. See what looks good in their photos before you start to figure out what would look good in *your* photo.

Then seek out photographers in your area—New York or L.A.— who specialize in shooting actors, and who have a good track record. Ask people in the business for recommendations, and check the ads in the trade papers (there are hundreds of ads, and most will reprint one or two sample shots to look at). Make appointments to visit and interview a few photographers, and ask to see their portfolios. There should be no hesitation when a photographer agrees to show you his or her work, and you should see a good selection of fine work. You should *like* the photos right off the bat, and not have to be talked into liking them. You should feel that, if you were a casting director, you would want to hire those people! You should want to be in that crowd. Ask the photographer some questions: Who's on his or her client list? How many *working* actors? How would he/she like to pose you? What does he/she think are your most photogenic aspects? What should you wear? Colors? Jewelry? The photographer is certainly no font of wisdom, but he or she should be comfortable answering your questions—and his or her answers should make sense.

Other things you might ask a photographer about include: What kind of camera would be used? *Studio* or view cameras were in vogue many years ago. They create a large negative, usually 4 x 5 inches and sometimes as large as 8 x 10, the size of the print itself, which produce prints of high technical quality (resolution or sharpness). The lighting and shading effects, as well as skin tone, can be subtle, and there's an opportunity to airbrush out some imperfections. The Karsh Studio of

Ottawa, for example, uses studio cameras, and many of its portraits are considered masterpieces.

More *candid* shots, on the other hand, are usually made with the smaller 35-millimeter or 2 1/4-inch film, which can provide much greater freedom (for the photographer) and naturalness (for you), in exchange for a modest loss in technical quality. Technical superiority in the studio shot, after all, can "read" simply as photographic staleness, which you certainly don't want. The candid head shot, consequently, is in more demand among actors today, in keeping with a freer and more lively notion of what great acting should be like.

Some head shots are shot outdoors; after all, films are frequently shot outdoors too. Outdoor photography can convey a vitality that rarely comes across in a posed studio photograph, no matter how carefully done. On the other hand, the lighting, background, and pose *must* read "professional" or all is lost—you are seeking to become a professional actor, not a mountaineer. The outdoor shot must be very carefully set up, and the photographer must have first-rate compositional skills. Anything that looks like a casual snapshot—a conflicting background, a smudged collar, a drooping eyelid—will be instantly relegated to the circular file (that is, tossed out).

You may at some time want a *composite photo*. This is a print that combines two or more shots of you, ordinarily in differing costumes or poses, into a single 8 x 10. Four poses are common in a composite (usually these are quarter-page 4 x 5s, evenly spaced), but some have five, six, or seven shots crammed in, using a combination of squares, circles, ovals, and rectangles. The idea is to show your various expressions, attitudes, and characteristics, in an eye-grabbing combination. Sometimes a composite leads with a master shot, larger than the rest, with surrounding smaller shots showing "what else you can look like." Other times the composite is printed on the flip side of a head shot. All this runs into considerably more money, of course. Any useful composite must be completed with great precision in the laboratory, so that the light levels in the various shots balance each other, the lines separating the prints are straight and even, and the overall composition is effective. Then the composite is usually lithographed or printed by photo-offset.

Head shot or composite? Get the head shot—except, possibly, for commercials. Virtually all theatre, film, and TV producers want the straight, uncomplicated head shot; it makes a bold, single impression, and that's what they're looking for. The casting director, after all, does not want to hire you for four roles, just one; a composite dilutes your

Sabrina La Rocca

Sabrina La Rocca   An exceptionally well done professional studio photo (note the highlight on the hair, and the way the face "jumps" off the page).   Photo: Larry Lapidus.

DAVID KOZUBEI

David Kozubei   A composite of four views of this well-recognized TV character.   Photo: Don Lewis.

BARBARA PASSOLT

Barbara Passolt   A very appealing and informal head shot of this fine young professional singer/actress, whose name appears in reverse (white) against her dark jacket.

look.   Even when you're auditioning for a repertory company, perhaps for multiple roles over a season, the casting director will want to see you as you are before thinking about what you will look like under makeup. Remember, the principal goal of your photographs should be to show you as *you are*. Agents and casting directors are virtually unanimous on this—if on little else.   Use only the makeup you would wear on an interview, if any, and allow no airbrushing; that which is beautiful, dramatic, sensitive, virile, or interesting in your appearance should appear to be coming from *you* rather than from some darkroom magician.

And *ask* the photographer.   In general, photographers who deal with actors have their own ideas about how you should be photographed and what sort of photos you should have.   They will also be happy to tell you which shots they prefer and which ones producers are likely to prefer.   They will make suggestions in posing and shooting you, and suggestions as to which contact prints should be enlarged.   Of course, a certain air of confidence is good business practice for the photographer as well, and the photographer is not trying for work, *you* are.   Still, a photographer's reputation comes from the actors he or she has photographed, who have gone on to successful careers, and any advice should be listened to with attention.

TAKING YOUR OWN PHOTOS

You may, of course, want to take your own photographs; photography is not, after all, a very mysterious art.   Perhaps you feel you have photographic talent, or maybe you haven't been able to find a good photographer, or maybe you just can't afford the going price for a sitting.   Why not give it a try?   Get a friend, a good camera and a telephoto lens (you can rent these for a day), and take a few rolls of black and white film down to the local park. If you come up with some good pictures, have them professionally processed and enlarged at a camera shop. Some actors even shoot themselves with a time-release button on the camera. Now, *most* homemade photos of this variety are pretty useless, because a fine photo involves careful attention to lighting, pose, background, angle, and composition, but if you are exceptionally talented and/or lucky, you might manage a classy, bright, intriguing picture. But don't settle for less. If you end up with nothing but a roll of snapshots, swallow your pride, dig into your wallet, and go to a pro. After all, you're about to become one yourself, aren't you?

FILM ON YOURSELF

It is more and more common for professional actors, particularly in Los Angeles, to have ten- to fifteen-minute VCR "demo" tapes available, as well as a book of still photographs. Ordinarily these should be tapes of professional work—a scene or a montage of scenes from your feature film or TV credits. You can often get a copy of such professional work by requesting it at the time you get the part. If you don't have professional tapes, there are services advertising in the trades that will make a demo for you, for $200 and up. The quality is no more than what you put into it, however. The industry-standard U-Matic 3/4-inch tape cassette is best for demos, but an ordinary household VHS 1/2-inch tape is increasingly being used. You can carry *both* formats in a carrying case, along with your book of still photos, for pulling out (and leaving off) at the right moment. Many studios advertising in the trades will be able to duplicate and transfer your demos, but *be sure to have extra copies* in case your tapes don't get returned in the shuffle.

RESUMES

Your resume is a listing of the parts you have played (and where, and—if impressive—with whom), printed on a single sheet, together with some basic information: your name; your telephone number (or, if you have an agent, your agent's number); your height, weight, hair and eye color; and your union affiliation, if any. Union affiliation is so important it should go right under your name, the magic letters being AEA, SAG, AFTRA.

There are also some occasional oddities you might mention at the bottom if you think they might be helpful in getting you work: who you trained with, what specialties you can do. "Tape available on request" announces you have film on yourself (see above). The resume is then stapled to the back of your photograph. Some photographers can actually print your resume on the back of your photo, but that's not, in fact, a very good idea. Your resume will need to be updated regularly (you hope!) and you won't want to have new photos printed each time.

Your resume should be carefully composed, professionally typed, and cleanly printed. While no actor ever got hired because of an expensive printing job on a photo-resume, and while superopulence can be an actual turn-off, *neatness* and *clarity* are very important; they indicate your professionalism.

There is no single format, but there are some general parameters you should stay within.

What information should you list on a resume? As to your physical characteristics, be honest. List your real—not your ideal—height and weight, or casting people will be mad when you turn out fatter or shorter than you led them to expect. Keep the description of your hair color up to date, if you go in for makeovers in that area. If you sing, give your vocal range. You don't need to list an age or an age range; your photo should show that adequately. Most casting directors feel that giving an age limits you more than it helps you. *If you are under 18,* however, give your *birth date,* as there are legal restrictions on your hiring that the casting people will need to know about beforehand. After 18, make new resumes.

As to your credits, your professional experiences are *by far* the most important ones. If you are in L.A., looking for film/TV work, then list film/TV work first; if you are looking for stage opportunities, head your resume with those. If you have acted with any union company, that credit should be listed above your amateur ones, even if the work was artistically inconsequential—if you have been an extra on a TV pilot, for example, put it above the Hamlet or Hedda you did in college. If you have acted with known stars, known directors, known actors, or known theatre companies, choose a format that highlights this information. Your resume is not a passive document, an application form to be faithfully filled out: It is a creative statement, an advertisement of your skills. Don't approach it as a duty but as art: a creative opportunity. If your experience is limited solely to college or school shows, list them proudly, and make them seem as if they were the most important shows done in the three-state area in which you lived.

But don't lie! Aside from moral reasons, you'll probably get caught. It's really a small world out there, and people do check. If you say you've acted for Peter Brook, the director who's interested in you might very well *call* Peter Brook to check you out; and if you really haven't, then you're in the muck. Or the person in the back of the room might *be* Peter Brook; you never can tell.

Want another reason not to lie? You'll be worrying the whole time that you'll be found out, and it will spoil your audition. Furtiveness and anxiety are disastrous for actors on an interview, and you only set yourself up for a sour stomach if you know you are presenting forged credentials.

MICHELLE FELTEN

Michelle Felten   An exceptionally well-designed resume, and an attractive, attention-getting head shot, presenting this not-yet-union performer in the best possible light.

MICHELLE FELTEN

C/O A.C.T.
450 Geary Street
San Francisco, CA 94102
(555) 555-5555

Height: 5' 3½"
Weight: 105
Eyes: Hazel
Hair: Brown
Voice: Mezzo-Soprano

AMERICAN CONSERVATORY THEATRE, San Francisco, CA
Mainstage

MARCO MILLIONS	Concubine	Joy Carlin

Studio

PERICLES	Thaisa	Scott Freeman
MAN OF MODE	Harriet	Kevin Jackson
ANTIGONE	Antigone	Steven A. Jones

Cabaret

ACT AFTER HOURS CABARET; "HOLLYWOOD MUSICALS"	John Johnson

PCPA THEATERFEST, Santa Maria, CA

. . . SUPERMAN	Lois Lane	Brad Carroll
SWEENEY TODD	Vermin	Jack Shouse
PUMP BOYS & DINETTES	Prudy (Understudy)	David Kazanjian

HILBERRY REPERTORY THEATRE, Detroit, MI

THE GREEKS	Cassandra/Electra	Robert McGill
AS YOU LIKE IT	Celia	Margaret Spear
THE GLASS MENAGERIE	Laura	Robert T. Hazzard

SRT SUMMER REPERTORY THEATRE, Santa Rosa, CA

THE SKIN OF OUR TEETH	Sabina	Phil Killian
I REMEMBER MAMA	Aunt Trina	Larry Hecht
A CHORUS LINE	Val	Rodger Henderson

RIVERFRONT PLAYERS, Spokane, WA

THE FANTASTICKS	Luisa	Dennis Craig

COEUR D' ALENE SUMMER THEATER, Coeur d' Alene, ID

EVITA	Mistress	Ralph McCoy
CABARET	Sally Bowles	Ralph McCoy
MAME	Agnes Gooch	Ralph McCoy

TRAINING
American Conservatory Theatre, Advanced Training Program
American Academy of Dramatic Arts, Pasadena, CA
Wayne State University, Detroit, MI, MFA Studies in Acting
B.A., Drama(UC Irvine), Workshops: Luis Valdez, Chris Villa
Dance: Lee Theodore(American Dance Machine); Jazz & Tap

SPECIAL SKILLS
Singing; Dance; Juggling; Combat; Professional Horseback Rider (English & Western).

ROBIN MELINDA McKEE

Robin McKee   Lists her personal manager's telephone on her resume, and pops her name boldly in reverse on her photo, which is casually styled.   Photo: William Gamble.

ROBIN MELINDA McKEE

SAG • AFTRA • AEA

Hair: Auburn
Eyes: Green
Height: 5'2"
Weight: 110 lbs.

Member of Theatre West
Singing Voice: Mezzo-Soprano/Belt

WAYNE GASSER
Personal Management/Public Relations
(555) 555-5555

TELEVISION & FILM

GOLDEN GIRLS	Featured	Dir.: Terri Hughes
IT'S GARRY SHANDLING'S SHOW	Featured	Dir.: Alan Rafkin
GUIDE TO GETTING GIRLS	Lead	Sargent-Reed Productions
FUTURE NEWS	Lead	Group "W" Cable T.V.
HOLLYWOOD DOCUMENTARY	Featured	French T.V. – Channel 4
WINTER SOLSTICE	Lead	KXTV – Channel 10 – Sacramento
EDUCATIONAL FILMS (3)	Lead	For the State of California

THEATRE

PEPPER STREET	Dolly Dazzle	Venture Theatre, L.A.
THE FREEDOM OF THE CITY	Balladier	Theatre West, L.A.
COLLAGE	Improv Comedy	Synthaxis Theatre Company, L.A.
THE TEMPEST	Ariel	Will Geer Theatricum Botanicum, L.A.
STARS IN HER EYES	Comet Mitchel	Synthaxis Theatre Company, L.A.
THE TAVERN	Sally (U/S)	Will Geer Theatricum Botanicum, L.A.
SIBLINGS	Samantha Lorenz	Callboard Theatre, L.A.
GOING TO SEE THE ELEPHANT	Sara	Sacramento Experimental Theater
WORKING	Housewife	The Village Theatre
BLIND RATS	Shirley	Sacramento Experimental Theater
THE MADWOMAN OF CHAILLOT	Constance	The Village Theatre
THE CANTERBURY TALES	Prioress	Premiere Theatre Company
LAUNDRY AND BOURBON	Elizabeth	The Village Theatre
OLD TIMES	Anna	The Studio Theatre
PATIENCE	Lady Jane	The Little Theatre

TRAINING

Acting: Gene Bua – Venture Theatre, L.A.
            Maria Gobetti – Victory Theatre, L.A.; Jeremiah Comey, L.A.
            M.A. in Theatre Arts – California State University – Sacramento
            The British Theatre Association
            B.A. in Drama – University of California – Irvine
Commercials: Beth Launer, L.A.
Voice: Allan Rich, L.A.
Dance: Ballet, Modern & Jazz – U.C. Irvine; The British Theatre Association

SPECIAL SKILLS

Classical & Rock Singer (14 years) – Comic Style & Comedy Singing – Instruments:
(Piano, Guitar & Dulcimer) – Voice-overs – Excellent Snow Skier – Tennis –
Aerobic Dance Instructor – Languages: (Fluent German & Conversational French) –
Dialects: (Southern, Cockney, High British, German & French)

90

COMMERCIALS **STA** (213) 555-5555 **Roger Michelson**
17502 PARTHENIA (818) 555-5555
NORTHRIDGE, CA 91325

Roger Michelson   A straightforward head shot, with the agent's logo, address, and telephone number prominently displayed to the left of the actor's name and on the resume as well.

R O G E R   M I C H E L S O N
SAG/AEA

COMMERCIALS
17502 PARTHENIA
NORTHRIDGE, CA 91325

Height: 6'3"
Weight: 195
Hair: Brown
Eyes: Hazel

FILM

State of Fear	Journalist	Stephen Cornwell (USC)
A Way of Life	Rick	Eric Elfman (UCLA)
Media	Justine Case	Eric Elfman (UCLA)
Summer Sunday	Martin Owen	Eric Elfman (UCLA)
Rent a Horse	Bill Smith	Vicki Rhoades (USC)
One Day in a Vampire's Castle	Dr. Seward	Vicki Rhoades (USC)

THEATRE

Singin' in the Rain	R.F. Simpson	Grand D.T. Anaheim
Cloud Nine	Harry/Edward	New Mexico Repertory
A Streetcar Named Desire	Mitch	New Mexico Repertory
A Midsummer Nights Dream	Demetrius	New Mexico Repertory
Hello Dolly!	Cornelius	Starlight, San Diego
Jailbirds on Broadway	Gary/Barry	Cast Theatre, L.A.
Annie	Bert Healy	Starlight, San Diego
Meet Me in St. Louis	Lon	Lawrence Welk Theatre
Oklahoma!	Curly	Mission Inn D.T.
Carousel	Billy	Mission Inn D.T.
Kiss Me Kate	Fred/Petruchio	Riverside, C.L.O.
Terra Nova	Robert F. Scott	Studio Theatre, Irvine
Picnic	Hal	Village Theatre, Irvine
Working	Steelworker	Concert Hall, Irvine
Bourgeois Gentleman	Cleonte	Village Theatre, Irvine

SPECIAL TRAINING

M.F.A. Acting, U.C. Irvine
B.A. Theatre, Cal State Long Beach
Acting: Robert Cohen (UCI), Bill Needles (Stratford Ontario, Canada),
      Jerzy Grotowski (Poland), Eric Kline, (Tony Barr), Bobby Hoffman.
Dialects and Speech: Dudley Knight.
Singing/Voice: Mahlon Schanzenbach.

At the bottom of your resume, you can include some miscellaneous information:

- Your special abilities (for example, performance sports, such as high diving or gymnastics, which you do superbly; circus acts; singing and dance experience; fencing skill; nightclub work; and so on)
- Your training in acting, singing, dance (listing the names of your instructors if they are well known outside your school)
- Languages you speak fluently, and dialects you can do fluently

Keep this "bottom" material to less than 10% of the resume.

You should *not* include the following kinds of information on your resume:

- Your interest or experience in directing or stage managing (it can be a turn off)
- Your membership in Phi Beta Kappa (ditto: "It doesn't do to be too smart. Actors who insist that they're brilliant—that puts you out of the running for half the roles you want to play," says Edward Herrmann[27])
- Your high school or college grades (nobody cares)
- Your hobbies (ditto)
- Your reasons for wanting a job (they know)
- Your dedication to acting (they know that too)
- Your willingness to do anything and everything (they'll find that out later if they cast you)
- Your psychological history (ditto)
- Your marital situation (it may change)

How cute should you be? Watch it. If you want to include a couple of humanizing details (such as your astrological sign or your ownership of wire-haired terriers), you might spark a conversation in an interview, but more likely you'll simply come off as an amateur. It's best to be simple, honest, effective, and businesslike, showing your experience at a glance.

Don't pad your resume. You can't make up for a lack of quality in your credits by substituting quantity. Actors who cram thirty-five amateur roles onto one sheet of paper only make it clear that they have been wasting away in the boondocks longer than has been good for them. It is better to show a half-dozen credits that look interesting than five dozen that look repetitious.

UNIONS

Your union affiliation, we have said, goes at the top of the resume. That may strike a note of terror in your mind—for how do you get into the union? You are probably already aware of the great "cycle of impossibility" that defines union membership: You can't get work until you are a member of the union, and you can't be a member of the union until you get work. Well, that's not true any more, not exactly. (It never was true, of course, it only *seemed* true.) You can get into the unions now somewhat more easily than in years back, but then union membership may not mean quite so much as it did then.

You have to understand, at the outset, that it's the *job* of unions to keep you out. That's one of the main reasons why there *are* unions: to keep you out of the picture (literally and figuratively). Unions protect their existing members, to whom you represent a threat—and, to be brutally frank, a cheap threat.

Remember, though, you will come to be happy there are unions. They will protect *you* if you become an actor. And if there were no actors' unions, actors wouldn't get minimum salaries, wouldn't get health benefits, wouldn't get fair working conditions, and wouldn't have retirement plans. Do you really think theatre owners would come up with retirement programs for actors on their own initiative? No, theatre owners have their hands full planning next year's season. The unions take care of the actors' long-range welfare. So the unions aren't the enemy, even though they may seem lined up against you at the beginning.

There are three principal actors' unions, already referred to often in these pages: the Actors' Equity Association (AEA, commonly called Equity), the Screen Actors Guild (SAG), and the American Federation of Television and Radio Artists (AFTRA). Equity, with 37,000 members, is the union for all stage actors; it's the oldest performer's union in America, founded in 1913, and has its main headquarters in New York, with branches in Los Angeles, Chicago, and San Francisco. SAG, which has its main offices in Los Angeles, has jurisdiction over acting in films and filmed television, including filmed television commercials. About half of SAG's 69,000 members live in the Los Angeles area, and the other half are served by about eighteen branch offices in cities across the country, including, of course, New York. AFTRA covers performers in live and videotaped television, including taped TV commercials. The 61,000 AFTRA members (half of whom are also in SAG) include, along with actors, all of TV's game show hosts, newscasters, sportscasters, and program announcers. As most soap operas are produced on videotape, daytime television is largely under AFTRA control. Radio announcers and performers also come under AFTRA's jurisdiction.

There is no accounting for the total number of actors in the three principal acting unions since many belong to two or three of them, but a good guess is that there are less than 100,000 unionized professional actors in all.

These three principal actor unions are joined by the Screen Extras Guild (SEG), the American Guild of Variety Artists (AGVA), and the American Guild of Musical Artists (AGMA) in the loose association known as the Associated Actors and Artistes of America (the Four "A's"). All these unions and guilds operate under American Federation of Labor–Congress of Industrial Organizations (AFL–CIO) charters, and SAG, particularly, emphasizes its AFL–CIO constituent status to achieve greater political clout than it could achieve on its own.

How can *you* join a union? Method one, the cleanest and most effective way by far if you can swing it, is simply to be offered an acting job by a union producer—that is, by a producer willing to sign you to a union contract. Sometimes the union will assess the producer a fine for doing that (as I said, the unions are not on your side yet), but if the director wants you badly enough, he or she will pay the fine (it can be $400 to $600) and you're in—this happens in every union almost every day. In that happy event, the union will be obligated to offer you membership, subject, of course, to your paying the hefty initiation fee ($500 for Equity, $632.50 for AFTRA, and $600 for SAG, in 1989), plus dues, which will be a minimum (Equity's is currently $52 per year) plus a percentage of your income. You can also join the union following six weeks of covered employment in an Equity company under a "mini contract" (used for certain off-Broadway shows), or for five presentations under a Theatre for Young Audiences (TYA) contract.

Method two is to join AFTRA, which since 1980 has been an "open union." This means you can join AFTRA simply by filling out an application and plunking down the initiation fee. SAG and Equity were horrified when AFTRA opened its membership to all comers, and they quickly withdrew the previously maintained right of AFTRA members to receive automatic entry into those two "sister unions." AFTRA membership, therefore, is easy to acquire, but useless as a "sister" stepping stone to SAG or Equity. It may even prove *harmful*, since it can be an obstacle to your joining Equity via method three.

That method three is Equity's *Membership Candidate Program*, which was initiated in 1978. The Program works this way: If you can secure certain acting or understudying work with a *participating Equity company*—the company may be under either LORT, CORST, COST, CAT, LOA, SPT, or dinner theatre contracts—you may register for this program with Equity. There is a $100 registration fee, which will eventually be counted toward your Equity initiation fee, and you must register on an official form the theatre company provides. Following your application, you will need to complete *fifty creditable work weeks* with the company, either in rehearsal and performance as an actor, or in rehearsal and performance as an understudy to an Equity role. In COST and CORST theatres, serving as production assistant to an Equity stage manager can count as well, as can ten weeks of other production work. The weeks need not be continuous, and you can add up weeks with different participating companies. You do not need to be paid for any of this work (that's up to you and the theatre company), nor is there any minimum number of lines or stage time required to qualify.

After your fifty creditable work weeks (or after forty such work weeks, plus passing an Equity-administered examination), you are eligible to join Equity simply by paying the initiation fee less your deposited $100 registration check. You will have five years in which to do this, after which your eligibility lapses. Note that nonresident aliens are not eligible for this program.

Equity recommends that your Membership Candidate application be filed as soon as you start your work. Your application is an affidavit of nonprofessional status, and certifies that you "are interested in obtaining training for the theatre and/or intend to make a career in the professional theatre." You can then list "Equity Membership Candidate" in the space on your resume where union affiliation goes; this is not union affiliation, but at least it's something.

Your "open" AFTRA membership, obtained by method two, may, as noted before, actually *prevent* you from becoming an Equity Membership Candidate! Equity looks dimly on AFTRA members who have signed into AFTRA without actually working, and requires such AFTRA (or even former AFTRA) members to make a "special request" for permission to join the Membership Candidate program. "This request should contain a copy of your resume and a detailed description of your professional work history," Equity states. Only after such a review will Equity waive your "method one" AFTRA card, and permit you to come aboard through the Membership Candidate Program.

The Membership Candidate Program is the best thing Equity has come up with in a long time. Unlike the earlier apprenticeship program, it *guarantees* union membership after a certain amount of work; the old program prevented the actor from remaining nonunion past a certain point, but it did nothing to ensure that the actor got a card. Equity has agreed to award credits retroactively in this new program for work performed since 1978 (1979 in dinner theatre), subject to application and approval.

Joining Equity through the Membership Candidate Program also (as of June 1, 1988) qualifies you as an *Eligible Performer* for all eligible performer auditions, which you will read about shortly.

Method four is to sidestep into one acting union by being a member of another. This is the "sister union" provision. If you are a fully paid up member of one acting union, have belonged to it for at least one year, *and have actually worked under its jurisdiction,* you may join either or both of the others. You can join Equity, for example, if you have done a principal or "under five" role as an AFTRA member, or three days of extra work as a SEG member, and filled the one-year requirement. That you must have actually *worked* under the parent union's jurisdiction excludes method-two AFTRA members from simply "sistering" in; AFTRA ensures that you understand all of this via a rider that you must sign at the time of joining.

Method five, which is not really a method at all, but which is the way most people make it, is to keep battering at the doors every way you can. You can be seen, you can be auditioned, and you can be cast professionally without being in a union, and without being an "eligible performer." It's harder, but it's obviously possible. It happens every day, and there's a lot of advice on how to do it in the pages that follow. There are doors that are closed, but there are always keyholes to peek through. Talent rises—and remember, if they find you and decide they want you, they'll hire you—they'll even pay a fine to hire you. Nobody's lack of union affiliation ever stopped a producer from trying to make a better movie, or a better play, or—let's face it—a bigger gross.

Eligible Performers

What's all this about Eligible Performers? A bit of history first: In the mid-1960s, Equity arranged with the various theatre producers that its members would have priority in auditions—indeed, that they would be *guaranteed* audition slots in an open call. Non-Equity actors under this arrangement would be seen, if at all, only after all Equity members had been auditioned.

All this changed very suddenly in April 1988, when, under a settlement with the National Labor Relations Board, Equity abandoned this policy, tacitly admitting its illegality. According to the settlement, "all actors who satisfy certain professional criteria, whether Equity members or not, will be treated in the same manner with respect to the scheduling of auditions." An "Eligible Performer" system has therefore been established to determine the "certain professional criteria." Under the new system, producers may not discriminate between union and nonunion actors, but they *can and will* discriminate between Eligible Performers (EPs) and ineligibles. What is an EP? How do you become one? You may qualify for an EP card if you fall into any of these three categories:

1. Actors (union or nonunion) who have performed before live theatre audiences for at least *four consecutive weeks*, receiving a salary equal to or higher than the minimum Equity salary (including benefits) for that period at that date, *or*

2. Actors (union or nonunion) who have made a salary equivalent to the above during any one calendar year by acting in film, television, or radio, *or*

3. *Apprentice* actors who have completed, since 1981, no less than *forty weeks* of stage performances, in professional theatres, before live audiences.

The minimum Equity salary you must have earned under categories (1) and (2) would, in 1990, have been $308 per week, or $1,236 for the four weeks. The qualifying sum depends on the year you earn (or earned) it, and the Equity minimum salaries that pertain (or pertained) at that time. For example, if you earned $207 a week for four consecutive weeks in 1982, or $105 a week for four consecutive weeks in 1973, you can qualify retroactively. If you earned your salary in 1989 or 1990, the sum will be a bit higher than stipulated here. The exact amount for ensuing years can be derived by taking Equity's smallest weekly minimum (which is currently for the TYA—Theatre for Young Audience—contract), plus the producer's required weekly contribution to Pension and Welfare Benefits under that contract, times two.

You will need to earn *no* money in category (3). This is the provision which makes Equity Membership Candidates, and some others as well, Eligible Performers.

You can become an EP, therefore, and receive priority treatment at all professional stage auditions without becoming a member of Equity—and, of course, Equity membership loses some of its cachet under this policy. All you need do is earn your $544 (or the adjusted figure for future years) as an actor for four consecutive weeks, in a theme park, for example, or earn that amount in one year acting in film or television. There are some catches. The payment must be a salary, not a fee; and taxes must be deducted as an indication of this. You should have a W-2 form, and/or appropriate documentation, to prove you did it. If you worked more than four weeks, you must have been paid at a uniform wage for each week. Also, the theatre must be professional, even if nonunion, with the majority of its performers paid. Community theatres, student theatres and films, and amateur theatres don't count. But performance work in many outdoor dramas, theme parks, dinner theatres, and Shakespeare Festivals can qualify you for EP status, and thereby for hundreds of open call auditions.

If you think you qualify, apply to Equity's Auditions Department. You will need an application form, proof of your qualifying earnings before live audiences (paychecks, contracts, playbills, and W-2 forms are mandatory), and, if you are approved, you will be billed a $12 processing fee. You will get an audition card that will admit you to any open EP call in New York, L.A., or Chicago. You will even be a step ahead of the 5% of Equity members who are *not* Eligible Performers.

Should You Join the Union?

Should you become an Eligible Performer? Yes, of course. It will make you eligible for hundreds of auditions a year you couldn't otherwise get into, and it costs you nothing but your $12.

Should you join a union? Yes—but . . .

It would be odd *not* to join the union if you had the chance, but there are some things to think about.

First, you must understand that being a member of the union means that you can *not*, in most circumstances, accept nonunion work.

Even finishing the Equity Membership Candidate program means this: Once you are in Equity, or have completed your fifty weeks as a Membership Candidate, you cannot, say, join the non-Equity acting company of a Shakespeare Festival. So you're left home by the telephone while your friends are braving the Bard in Oregon or Lake Champlain.

As a union member, your hands are a bit tied; and please don't try acting under a false name, either—you'll be caught and disciplined.

You may also not be able to afford the initiation fee: $500 for Equity, $600 for SAG, and $632.50 for AFTRA. Plus dues.

If you want to keep your options open, you need *not* join a union right away, even if you complete your fifty weeks, and even if you get a union job. The Candidate Program gives you five years, remember, before you have to join. And a provision of the Taft-Hartley Law allows you to accept up to thirty consecutive days of fully professional work without having to join any union. But on the thirty-first day of work in a union-authorized production, you *must* join—or retire.

Probably, though, you will want to join at the first opportunity.

First of all, you're going to join anyway; you might as well do it when you get the chance. Secondly, you're going to want to support the efforts that will make your professional life easier: efforts to negotiate minimum wages and maximum working conditions, for example. And you're going to want to have easy access to the information sources that unions provide, including their own magazines, lobbies, bulletin boards, hot line telephone numbers, seminars, meetings, and informal networking services.

Where a union card will give you priority status in auditions, that's a plus too. Union (SAG) membership is still a virtual necessity in the film industry (although the NLRB is taking a hard look at SAG as well). And Equity membership still has a strong cachet for stage producers, though they have equal legal obligations to the EPs. Habits are slow to change in this business.

But the main factors concerning union membership might be psychological. An Equity or SAG card makes you feel better about yourself and your career, and if you feel better you'll probably act better. Remember that "talent" is largely self-confidence, and card-carrying unionism, in this field, breeds professional pride. Rightly or wrongly, you'll walk a bit taller, and probably look a bit larger in other people's eyes as well. The fact is that most folks in show business simply assume, probably at the unconscious level, that only union membership conveys "big league" status, and that nonunion actors

(EP or otherwise) are somewhere in the "minors." That's hardly the truth—or hardly the entire truth—but why fight it when you've got so many other battles yet to win?

AGENTS AND AGENCIES

No character in the theatre or film industry arouses such contradictory attitudes as the agent. To the beginning actor, without contacts and without credits, the agent appears as a savior: the ultimate path to fame, fortune, and career. Actors fall all over themselves trying to get an agent to "represent" them, to "submit" them, to demonstrate their brilliance to the casting moguls, to do their hatchet work, spade work, telephoning, and interviewing.

But to the established actor, the agent is often the devil incarnate, the ubiquitous middleman with no interests—artistic or personal—but the inevitable 10% cut. A famous actor once paid his agency a commission of more than $10,000 in pennies, hauled up in an armored truck. Lawsuits and contract-breaking between actors and their agents are unfortunately common in this volatile industry. K. Callan begins both of her excellent books, *The N.Y. Agent Book* and *The L.A. Agent Book* (1987 and 1988, respectively) with discussions on why you should *leave* your agent. Dishonesty, lack of communication, failure to be sent out, and persistent thoughts of suicide head Callan's list. Also theft: "Stealing your money is a sound reason to leave. Stealing your trust is another."[28]

Most agents are somewhere between saviors and thieves, however. For actors, the agent is at least an invaluable aid, and at most (particularly in Hollywood) a virtual necessity. So it's necessary to understand the agent—and agency—function.

An agent (the word comes from the Greek *agein*, "to drive") pushes forward (yes, "drives") your career, making his or her own income solely to the extent he or she helps you make yours.

The agent's job is to get you employment, and to negotiate the best possible salary for you. In return, the agent earns a percentage of what you do, ordinarily 10% of what you get through the agent's overtures. The agent *does not charge a fee* (if an agent proposes a fee, he or she isn't an agent!). If you don't work, the agent doesn't get paid, which creates some incentive for the agent to produce on your behalf. Even the 10% commission doesn't always kick in at lower income levels: in SAG-AFTRA work, the union will require you to be paid at least 10% more than "scale" so your agent's commission won't drag your fee down below minimum SAG standards. In Equity work at low-paying theatres (LORT B and below, off-Broadway, and so on), the agent's commission doesn't get paid until after ten weeks of performances; up to that time the agent gets a nominal flat rate ($50 to $100, depending on the theatre's size). This is one of the reasons why agents aren't as involved in stage work as they are in film: They don't get paid as much, or as often. Agent's fees aren't going to break your back, then, as a beginner, and you should certainly seek such a valuable business partner.

The role of agents and agencies and their importance varies significantly between New York and Hollywood, and between stage and camera actors. In New York, the agent is an important factor in most casting situations; in L.A. the agent is *crucial*. In Los Angeles, you simply *must* have an agent, preferably one with whom you have a signed, exclusive contract, in order to get serious work in films or television. In New York, the situation is quite a bit freer, and the relationships between agents and actors is considerably less formal. In New York you may be represented by several agents, but on an unsigned, free-lance basis.

What does an agent do for you? Basically, the agent "submits" you for private auditions—at film studios, with Broadway producers, and for television. These are not auditions that are posted anywhere, but rather auditions the agent knows about through private sources, mainly through trade-circulated "breakdowns." No, this has nothing to do with a mental collapse, though these are common in this business. The Breakdown Service is a product available to agents only; it lists and describes all the roles—by sex, age, and character type—in upcoming TV episodic and movie-of-the-week scripts, and in a good number of Broadway plays and feature film scripts as well. Obviously, to an actor, these breakdowns are worth their weight in platinum, and they cost almost as much. But you can't see them—not legally, anyway. Agents buy them, and in buying them agree in writing not to show them to their actor clients. Breakdowns help the agents focus their submittals, and narrow the range of actors they will submit for each role.

The agent also can arrange private interviews for you with casting directors and other casting people. Obviously these will be several steps above the cattle call situations that your Eligible Performer card will admit you to.

Why can't you arrange all these auditions and interviews yourself? Why can't you just "submit yourself"? Because:

1. you don't have the breakdowns, so don't know the parts,

2. you don't have the contacts, so don't know the casting people, and

3. you don't have the credentials, since most casting people won't usually see you until an agent verifies that you're worth seeing.

So, you want—and probably need—an agent to represent and submit you. Generally you want a formalized agency arrangement, usually with an exclusive contract (always in L.A.; more often than not in New York). Your agent will take your photographs or make you get new ones, and will have you redo your resumes with the agency name and phone number as your contact; your new photo-resumes will become the calling cards for your submittals.

Your agent will then search through the breakdowns, and whatever other casting information is available to the agency. (Lots of scripts never turn up in the breakdowns, and lots of parts are written into TV shows at the last minute; a good agent is always hustling for this kind of information.) Then the agent will submit you to the appropriate producers or casting director for projects you might have a crack at getting into.

If a casting person bites, he or she will call the agent, the agent will call you, and an interview and possibly an audition will be set up—not necessarily at your convenience, of course. You will be given whatever information the agent can get about the part (a SAG rule, rarely enforced, says you must have 24 hours lead time to read the script—but the script may not be ready in time), and sometimes, if you are a particularly favored client, or the agent has the time and thinks it would be a good idea, your agent may personally escort you to the interview, introduce you to the producers, and try in other ways to grease the machinery for you. At that point, however, you are on your own. The interview and audition both depend on you. If you come through with flying colors and the casting people want you, somebody will call the agent back.

Here's another critical step. Your agent and a producer will negotiate your salary; surprisingly, perhaps, you may find you have little to say about it. If all goes well, your agent will get you the best salary the producer is willing to offer; the agent will then call you and tell you the terms.   When you get paid you give your agent whatever percentage of your gross income (the income paid to you before taxes are deducted) that your agency contract specifies.

So the actor-agent relationship is a good one when it works, and much of the time it *does* work. You are spending your time perfecting your craft, and your agent is hustling up and down Sunset Boulevard or Seventh Avenue looking for your future job.

But, of course, there are the inevitable wrinkles.

The agent can ignore you. An agent can take you on with marvelous promises, take a hundred photos and resumes, and never call you again. When this happens you question why the agent took you on in the first place. What may have happened is that you have a highly unusual look and the agent simply wanted to file your pictures away until a call came in for just that look—and the call never arrived. Or the next day the agent may have found someone just like you but "better." Or the agent may have had other designs on your company which you, unwittingly, did not oblige (it's a real world out there, folks). There can be *any number* of reasons why an agent takes you on and then ignores you, and it happens all the time. That's why Ms. Callan begins her book on how to get an agent with advice on how to leave one. If you haven't signed a contract, you've lost nothing but your photos; just start looking for somebody else. If you've signed a contract, you've got to start pushing your agent to get on the stick. Standard Hollywood agency contracts allow you to terminate your representation if you have not received 15 days work in the past 91 days (in New York, it's in the past 120 days), but if the agent isn't working out, you can probably negotiate an amicable withdrawal sooner than that.

The agent can promote you for the wrong roles. Agents are not simply clearing offices, they are second-guessers. They do their own breakdowns, of course; you've got to make sure they don't break *you* down. "I admit, we play God," confesses one. Well, they *have* to. An agent can't send fifty clients for a single reading—he or she would never get a call again. Remember, most agents know what they're doing; most are *objective* about your chances, and most probably know how to market you best. But sometimes they don't.

(You may be offended at the terms agents use: You are part of their "stable" of talent, you are "marketed" like a cabbage, you are a "juvenile female" instead of an actress—you will have to learn to live with this, too.)

The agent can be too greedy on your behalf. An actor who sings and plays the guitar was offered a terrific contract at a prestigious New York nightclub, where many celebrities got their starts. He had, however, recently signed with an agent who persuaded him he should get more money. He demanded what she said, the offer was withdrawn, and he never had the chance again. (Shed no tears; he now directs "Who's the Boss?") Other agents go well beyond persuading you to overreach your salary potential; they demand it in your name without even consulting you. Since the agent bargains directly with the producer before you do, your agent can keep you out of roles you have successfully auditioned for. No matter that you would work for free in order to get that first credit. Your agent may negotiate you right out of it by demanding an extra $100. You may see this as just the chance you take—after all, the agent is interested in the same thing you are, right? Not exactly. The agent is interested in your *income*, which is not always the same as your total artistic and career growth. The best agents are interested in that, too; the greedy ones want their cut and they want it now. Sympathize with them; they have big phone bills. But be alert. Your best interests and theirs are not always exactly the same. You have the final option, if you demand it. Gary Shaffer, casting director for "Dynasty," "Trapper John," and various movies-of-the-week, advises, "If you want to be an actor, have your agent submit you for everything. Don't worry about pay. Tell him not to turn down *anything*."

Finally, an agent can simply give you bad advice. In that, the agent is no more guilty than anybody else you may come across, but it hurts more when your agent advises you badly because you feel obligated to take the advice. In fact, you probably *are* obligated to take it if you want the agent to help you. But the agent is not always the most objective observer of the industry. Remember that agents are often former (or failed) actors, and sometimes they have their own axes to grind—and they may just grind them on you. They may also be in a bad mood; understand that despite their savior status in some aspirants' minds, agents do not live a very heavenly life. They spend most of their time nagging casting people, bugging receptionists for scraps of information, and being put on HOLD; sometimes they will take their frustration out on their clients, which means on you. So, in their offices, *they* know all the answers: how you should act, what your pictures should look like, what acting teacher you should study with, how right you are for what role, and how much weight you should lose. Now, in all honesty, your agent is *probably* right. But the *degree* of probability is not as great as most agents would have you believe.

Knowing the wrinkles, should you try to get an agent? Of course, you should. The agent is on the inside of the business and you aren't. Some are more careful, likable, honest, and well known than others, but all franchised agents have access to important contacts and information that you don't. In New York, most important casting is done through agencies; in Hollywood virtually *all* casting is. In Hollywood, indeed, the agent has virtually become a producer, so involved have the agencies grown in packaging and planning film and television productions. Some of the most important studio chiefs in Hollywood—for example, David Begelmen at MGM and Louis Wasserman at Universal—are, in fact, ex-agents. Forget the cigar chomping, ex-vaudevillian image; Hollywood agents now tend to be college graduates and business people; they are the power brokers of the film world.

Finding and Getting an Agent

There are literally hundreds of agents and agencies in both L.A. and New York (there are some in other cities as well, though not of similar importance), and agencies vary enormously in their practical worth—particularly for an actor who's starting out. The difference between having a career and not having one can quite easily depend on which door you knock on first.

Many agents work in their own offices and handle an absolute minimum of clients. One, for example, handles only six. You needn't worry about him, though; four of those six make more than $3 million a year. The other two are expected "comers." Obviously that is the kind of agent you want. Also, obviously, that is not the kind of agent you're going to get. Not yet, anyway.

Other agents work in the huge prestige "star" agencies, of which there are five: William Morris, Triad, APA (Agency for the Performing Arts), ICM (International Creative Management), and CAA (Creative Artists Agency). The star agencies have offices in both New York and Los Angeles; each office may have 50-75 agents who handle the affairs of up to 2,000 actors, a lot of whom are the people you have heard about since you were 12. It may do your ego good to be contracted by the same agency that "handles" Jack Nicholson, Sylvester Stallone, and Barbra Streisand (not to mention Gerald Ford and Ted Kennedy), but remember that a big agency has big clients, and 10% of Stallone's income means a lot more to them than 10% of yours. For this reason, the big agencies never (well, almost never) even look at an actor who isn't already well established and making a sizable income. When you figure that a major agent must book a million dollars worth of business to pay secretaries, rent, and alimony, and have anything left over for profit, you will realize that only hungry agents are going to take you on when your expectations are still in the range of subsistence wages.

For a beginning actor, it is almost certainly best to ignore the bigger agencies (which will ignore you in any event) and to hunt out the small, aggressive, hungrier operations that look at untried talent and have the time and inclination to develop a genuine interest in your development. Only then will the actor–agent relationship—a marriage in many ways—prove truly fruitful.

How do you pick an agent to call? First of all, the agent must be franchised. In Hollywood this means franchised at least by the Screen Actors Guild, and in New York by the Actors' Equity Association—but preferably your agency should be franchised by all three unions. Any of the three union offices will give you lists of their franchised agents (sometimes for a nominal charge), and under no circumstances should you sign with a nonfranchised one; franchised agencies will have a license on the wall. Beware: Phony "talent agencies" spring up every year, charging fees (no legitimate agent charges any fee), or requiring you to use the company photographer (usually somebody's brother-in-law) and/or to attend a "class" or "workshop" prior to signing on. These are positively *illegal*: Franchised agencies may not require that you use specified photographers, nor may they operate schools. Alert the appropriate union if you are approached for this scam. The state labor commissioner will do something about it.

So you have a list of franchised agents. Still, a list is only a list, and it will be an unwieldy one: There are simply hundreds of agencies. You will need to do some winnowing down.

First, if you have friends in the industry, ask them for suggestions. Can someone recommend an agency to you? Beyond that, can they recommend you to the agency?

Check out the agency *ratings* books listed in the appendix (the K. Callan books, the Dennis Haskins book, and the annotated listings published by Acting World Books are a good start). Make your own list of possible agents to contact on the basis of what you read there.

Thumb through the pages of the *Players Directory* in Hollywood, or the *Players Guide* in New York (we sent you there in the "Photos" section, above), which will show you the working actors in both cities, with the names of their agents. Check out the agencies that seem to employ actors of your type. You will certainly get, from this exercise, some sort of picture of which agents are handling which kinds of clients, and you will get a sharper idea of where to start.

From these sources you should be able to find the names of ten to fifteen smallish agencies that handle people like yourself and might be interested in taking on new clients. Perhaps you can rank them in order of desirability, particularly if any of them have been especially recommended by someone you trust. And then you must call on them.

Agents are busy people, and they are not always going to be eager to see you if you just pop in and announce yourself. Some, particularly in New York, have open interview hours each week. Most do not, and *all* have a standard set of procedures to dissuade casual drop-ins and phone calls. Unless you do things the right way, you usually won't get past the receptionist. Here, then, are the time-honored ways, in order of their effectiveness, of making that first appointment.

Use a personal contact. There is that dirty word again—sorry, but it's more important here than ever. The biggest agents won't see *anybody* without some personal reference, and a personal reference from somebody important at that. Your best chance of getting an agent, if you can swing it, is to be recommended by a working producer. And get the *producer* to set up the appointment if you can (if you can't, at least get permission to use the producer's name, and an understanding that the agent can call the producer to verify). If a producer is behind you, the agent will feel that you already have a leg up on getting work; besides, by taking you on, the agent may be able to broaden his or her *own* contacts at the same time. Remember, like you, the agent is always looking for ways to strengthen contacts. But even if the contact is just another actor who recommends that you see his or her agent (which, ordinarily, only an actor of the opposite sex is likely to do), the personal contact is an invaluable way to get your foot in the door.

Your second way to an agent's office is by mail: a good cover letter, making clear your immediate availability, together with your photo-resume. You can make a mass mailing to all the agents in either town, using preaddressed mailing labels available for a modest charge in the drama bookshops in both New York and L.A. (see the appendix). With a smashing photo, and/or outstanding professional credits, you can often get an interview on the spot. Arthur Rosenberg, a fine character actor, came to Hollywood with five years of solid LORT credits on his resume. He sent photo-resumes to the more than 200 agents then in Hollywood, and received seventeen invitations to interview. This led to two offers to sign. You only have to do half as well as Rosenberg, since it only takes *one* offer to get an agent—but his extensive professional credits were crucial.

If you lack a personal contact or extensive professional credits, your next best means of landing an agent is to be *seen* in something. This involves getting a fairly good role in a "showcase." The name says it all. You are paid little or nothing (you may even have to pay), but you are "showcased," put on display for all comers. Showcases come in many forms: nearby regional productions, New York's off-off-Broadway productions, L.A.'s old "Equity-waiver" or "99-seat the-atre" productions (so-called because they are performed by profes-sionals without salary, or at less than scale wages, under a waiver from Equity that applies to theatres with fewer than 99 seats), and just plain amateur productions, sometimes those that you pay to participate in. The latter are formal showcase theatre companies, which you join; your monthly dues make you a member of their casting pool. Show-case theatre companies are particularly popular in L.A.: Theatre 40, the Colony Theatre, and the Group Repertory Theatre are among the better known ones. Some drama schools also present L.A. and/or New York showcases for their graduates to perform in, inviting profes-sional agents and casting directors to attend. It doesn't matter who produces the showcase, but it does matter who comes. The test of a showcase is the number of agents and casting people who actually arrive and see the show. Ticket prices should be low, comp tickets generously given, and the industry audience should be assiduously courted.

Getting a good part in a showcase is not by any means automatic, but you can quickly find your way around to their auditions. In New York, trade papers and the *Village Voice* are good sources of informa-tion about the off-off-Broadway market; in Los Angeles, *Drama-Logue* will let you know what is going on. When you get your showcase role, you should do everything you can to attract attention (that's the whole point of doing it)—so print up and mail out flyers and invitations (you can print your photos on these if you want), solicit RSVPs, send photo-postcard reminders, arrange limousine transportation for reluctant agents (some showcases provide valet parking and buffet meals!), and even pay for advertisements in the trade papers. Follow-up is crucial. If you get good trade reviews, you can print up new photo-postcard invitations, highlighting your reviews, and send out a second round. Showcases should always record the industry people who attend (ordinarily a sign-in book is provided in the lobby); all of these should get a follow-up letter from you—and, if all else fails, a phone call. If you're good and have professional potential, they'll get back to you.

Agents and casting people do see showcases, some as often as three or four a week. Showcases are your best first way of getting seen at *work*, and paid work really does come out of them if you touch all the right bases.

Interviewing an Agent

Once you have an agent interested in you, you'll probably be asked in for an interview. The interview is crucial; it will determine if the agent takes you on. Since you will also be interviewing for roles later on, you must treat the interview with the agent just as seriously as an interview with a producer or director. The agent will be trying to see if you interview as well as you act, and it is important that you do.

If you are invited to "come in and talk," set up an appointment and keep it exactly. Arrive on time, and look your best. Be yourself, but be clean, neat, and striking. "Look like an actor and act like an actor," suggests one agent. Be at ease and be positive. Agents aren't necessarily any good at interviewing; they may be awkward and nervous just like you. *Help* the agent interview you. Don't just wait for questions: Describe your career, your desires, your commitment, your training, what you feel you can do, and what sacrifices you are prepared to make. Don't ham it up, but be active, infectious; obviously an agent will be more interested in you if it appears that you have what it takes to generate a career.

Impress the agent that you want to become a working professional actor, and that you have a realistic outlook about the business, and about your future. Don't presume to know more about show business than the agent does, and don't fret openly about your recent failures, whatever they may be. Offer to audition; most agents will see an audition in their office, and you should have a monologue prepared. Offer to come back in with a scene—but have a rehearsed scene and scene partner ready for just such occasions.

Ask some questions, too. How does the agent see you? How does the agent see using you? Each agent has a particular point of view, and an agent whose plan to use you doesn't ring the bells may prove worse than no agent at all. You want an agent who, regardless of his or her standing, is enthusiastic about you, and sees you pretty much the way you want to be seen. If you want to play classical tragedy and the agent wants to sell you for soap opera, you had better get things straight before you sign. No agent will be offended if you simply ask:

"How do you see me?" Let him or her tell you; you may be astonished at what you hear. Give your agent the benefit of the doubt, if there is one. You might, amazingly, prove to be a lot better in "As the World Turns" than in *As You Like It*. On the other hand, you may not want to spend the rest of your life in the soaps, so you have some decisions to make.

Close the interview when you think you have said and asked everything on your mind. Know when to quit talking, and offer to leave (it's best to be leaving "for an audition at Universal" than "for an appointment at the dentist's").

The agent will probably *not* offer you a contract on the spot. He or she may want to think you over, to consult with colleagues, and to check the files for available jobs in your line. If the agent doesn't grab you on the way out, he or she might well call you later. Your task is simply to hang in there until something happens.

And then it does happen: An agent decides to take you on as a client. In Hollywood you will sign an exclusive contract for the agent to represent you in all *dramatic* camera media. Later you may get another agent for commercials, and yet another for live theatre, although some agents will handle all three. In New York you *may* be asked to sign an exclusive contract, or the agent may simply take you on as a free-lance client, in which case you can work with several agents.

Should you sign up or free-lance? It's probably best to sign—that way, the agent is more committed to you, and you to the agent. Also the agent will probably think of you before going to his or her free-lance list. An agent who sends a free-lancer up for a role first has to confirm the submission with the actor, to make sure that the actor hasn't already been submitted by another agent; this takes time, and the agent may not want to bother with the extra phone call. But signing up is also signing away; it's a major career decision, something like a marriage, and you should feel pretty good about it before going ahead.

When you sign with an agent, you have entered into a partnership you both hope will prove beneficial to both of you. But *you have by no means "made it"*; you are still just beginning.

A good agent will take a serious interest in your career. He or she will get your pictures into the *Players Directory* or *Players Guide* (though you will probably pay the fee), and will seek out casting opportunities, through breakdown services and other sources available only to agencies. The agent will, to some extent, be the manager of your career—

even if you have a manager (see below). It is vital, therefore, that you establish a trusting relationship. This may take some patience on your part. One agent cautions, "It may take a year or so to establish you in the overall market picture, and another two years to get offers coming in with any regularity. The third year is usually when the payoff comes—if it does." If you are hoping for instant results, you may be very frustrated. Actors who impatiently switch agents every six months only have to begin over and over again, and never establish an image in the industry.

If you are lucky enough to find an agent who sees you the way you wish to be seen, an agent in whom you feel confident, sign up and follow the agent's advice. Accept his or her judgment on your photographs, what you should wear, how you should do your hair, how much weight you should lose, and so forth. Talk things over, but be prepared to trust. Nobody's advice is perfect, but your agent is your partner, and the two of you should be working together, or not at all.

And don't settle back! Just because you have an agent, you can't afford to become a passive participant in your own career. You are still going to have to make your rounds, get yourself known, get involved, and generate your network of contacts. You're also going to have to energize your own agent! As William Bayer explains, "Hustle your hustler. You're going to have to sell and pressure and hustle just as much with an agent as without one; you're going to have to continue to excite your agent, because the moment he gets bored, there's nothing in it for either of you."[29] Exasperating? Yes, but true. Your agent needs reinforcement when he puts your name out there. He or she needs casting people to *glow* at the mention of your name, not stare blankly in quizzical puzzlement. And that means getting known—making your rounds.

MANAGERS

Should you have a manager? Some actors now turn to personal managers and business managers to advise them in their careers. Managers do not replace agents (a manager cannot negotiate a contract, only a franchised agent can), so your fee to the manager, which is usually 15% of your income and can include a flat fee besides, is *in addition* to your agent's commission. And most of what a manager will do should be done by your agent anyway. Ordinarily, then, you should *not* get involved with a manager. But there are some exceptions; some people who should have a manager; these include: (1) very successful actors, who need business guidance, (2) actors in whose future a potential manager has made a substantial cash proposition, and (3) actors for whom the manager offers valuable services available no other way. There are, certainly, occasions when a manager will be so skilled, so enthusiastic and committed on your behalf, and so successful in making and using professional contacts to benefit your career, that his or her help will prove vital. Finding when this situation exists, however, is the trick—and it's a puzzler. What professional contacts does a manager really have? Show business, remember, is name-dropper land. You might need to hire a professional investigator to find this one out. Best to avoid a manager, unless very compelling evidence suggests the reverse.

ROUNDS: SEEING THE CDS

What do actors do when they are not working? They go on rounds. This is as time-honored as the opening night party at Sardi's. It means going to see everybody and anybody who can get them a job in the theatre. These days, it basically means going to see casting directors.

The casting director is a relatively new creature in the theatrical world, brought into existence, among other reasons, by the fact that there are just so many of you (actors) out there that directors and producers don't have the time to find out about you—they're too busy directing and producing.

Casting directors (CDs) are hired by the major studios, by individual film and television production companies, by Broadway producers, and by some regional theatres. Sometimes they are part of a permanent staff (as at the Universal Studios casting department); more often they are free-lancers, with their own New York and L.A. offices, hired for individual projects. Their job is to recommend, out of the hundred thousand or so professional actors, the two or three that the director and producer will want to see. You want to be in that two or three, naturally.

It is the CD's goal to find the best talent for the project or company he or she is working for. It's your goal to convince the CD that that's you, but the CD has to see you first.

Casting directors *want* to know the work of every actor in the business; it's their *job* to know you if you're any good, and it's also their job to know how to get in touch with you. They go to showcases all the time, therefore, as well as to screenings and theatre productions (Broadway, off-Broadway, LORT, depending on where they're located), and they also watch television—they probably watch more television than anybody in the business.

They also see actors in their own casting offices when they have time, and your rounds are basically rounds of those offices. Most CDs give general office auditions, and the first step in your rounds is to write all the casting directors in town—in New York or L.A. that is— and ask for an appointment. Your letter should be brief but interesting, and your photo-resume should be a grabber. Your agent, if you have one, will help you with all this, but you can often see a CD without an agent; you can write to a CD directly for an interview, just as you write to an agent.

Trade bookshops on both coasts have preaddressed mailing labels for all the CDs in each town, and Wendy Shawn's *L.A.'s & N.Y.'s Casting Directors* (see the bibliography) has a well-developed (and regularly updated) list, annotated as to which CDs give general auditions, as well as an indication of what individual CDs are looking for. The L.A.-based *CD Directory* and the N.Y.-based *Ross Reports* are even more comprehensive, although not annotated.

Your CD interview is likely to be similar to an agent's interview, and you should be prepared to present an audition; it's a good idea to have a couple of pieces ready (see the next section.) You should also be prepared to show a book of photos, or (better) some "film on yourself," meaning a ten- or fifteen-minute videocassette demo, preferably from a feature film or network TV show. (See "Photos," above.) Have extra copies of your demo: The CD may ask to hang onto your tape for a few days to show someone else. Don't forget to put your name, address, and phone number on it, too; some actors even hand them out in self-stamped, self-addressed return mailers.

Do you go on CD rounds even though you have an agent? Absolutely—the agent can help you only so far; the ultimate initiative must be yours, and you have to keep at it. "If you stop pushing for one minute, they forget you. You're out. Gone, goodbye," says actress Terri Garr. Don't wait to be asked, go for the interview; audition! A casting director described a particularly successful actor:

> He works a lot because he *never* stops plugging. He makes job hunting a full-time occupation. He has an excellent agent, but he gets himself one-half of his jobs! Everyday he goes to one studio, dropping by to just say "hi" to the casting people, so he

will be fresh in their minds. He reads the trades every day to see what new projects are beginning and who is involved. He then immediately goes to see them, no matter how big they are (both Robert Wise and Mike Nichols have thrown him out of their offices!). He's got a lot of *chutzpah*—a true necessity. He marches right through (or drives right through) the studio gates: You can go *anywhere* if you look like you belong, so simply wave at the studio guard.

So rounds become your day-to-day lifestyle in New York or Hollywood.

Since you are literally going to be seeing *hundreds* of agents and CDs in your first year in the business, you should *log* your rounds. Some actors do this in a notebook, others in a card file. Your log should list the date you submitted each photo-resume, and where; the date you visited each agent and casting office; the names of the people you spoke with, and their suggestions for following up, if any. You will want to pay repeat visits to some agencies, but you will have to space these out so as not to become a pest. Don't count on your memory for very much, because you can visit and forget dozens of offices a day, and come home with only the foggiest idea of where you've been or what you've accomplished.

CD Workshops, Classes, and Seminars

It has recently become the fashion for CDs to offer, at a price, workshops and seminars in auditioning, and showcases to which other CDs are invited. These activities are in sort of a gray area morally, for while the CD clearly is able to offer you sound advice on how to audition, you are also, quite obviously, paying to be seen, and paying the person you hope will hire you. This comes awfully close to bribery—yet it is generally conducted in an above-board manner, and work does come out of it. You should investigate these seminars carefully, and make certain you are actually getting your money's worth *in instruction* before signing on. You should also check the CD's credentials; after all, anyone can *claim* to be a CD, and yet be just as much an unemployed beginner as you are. (CDs, unlike agents, are not franchised.) The fees for such workshops should also be in line with other such professional classes advertised in the trades; if they're substantially above that, take a *very* close look.

GETTING KNOWN: ADVERTISEMENTS
FOR YOURSELF

With or without an agent, and with or without a union card, you must get known and get seen. You must advertise yourself. Making rounds is a form of self-advertisement. So is getting your picture into the *Players Guide* or *Players Directory*, although you must have your union card to get into either of them (to get into the *Directory* you must also be represented by a SAG-franchised agent). "We open that book a hundred times a day," says Jerold Franks, casting director for Columbia Pictures, referring to the *Directory*. [30] An actor can have one or two pictures published in the *Directory*; it costs (in 1989) $15 per issue, per category (if you go in as both an ingenue and a leading lady, you will pay twice the fee). That's $45 for the year, per category (there are three issues); comparable rates admit you to the once-a-year New York *Guide* (addresses in the appendix).

Photo-postcards make effective quickie advertisements that can circulate your picture under the guise of an otherwise ordinary communication. Your photo and name, printed on one side, accompanies your message (and the address of the person to whom you're writing) on the other. Such postcards, which you can have made in bulk, are a good way to confirm dates, thank people for their attention and consideration, and announce your current activities to those who've expressed some interest in hearing about them. Postcards also have the advantage of being easily thumbtacked to a wall if anybody wants to look at you for a day or two—and who knows but that they might?

Then there's the bolder approach. Advertise in print. The most discreet advertising is done by stars, who pay high fees to take space in *Variety* to "congratulate" the magazine on its anniversary (and make clear the star is still alive, kicking, and available). Stars also become the spokespersons for charities that will keep their name before the public, and raise the moral standard of their reputations.

You probably can't become a charity spokesperson yet, but an ad promoting your successful appearance in a showcase is very worthwhile. Elaine Partnow, a Los Angeles actress, capitalized on her performance in a workshop production by using some of her reviews, which were in the "brilliant" category, to put together a quarter-page ad in (Daily) *Variety*. Then she made up 800 reproductions of the ad and sent them to every producer and director in television, and every Equity theatre in the country. The result: two phone calls. At $200 a call, that's an expensive way to get known, but two phone calls are, after all, better than none. And you're not limited to postcards and quarter-pages, either. One Alma Kessler paid $10,000 to put her face (six times life-size) on billboards over Sunset Boulevard, with the leading line "Who is Alma Kessler and what's her game?" "Why did you do it?" she was asked. "I love show business," she replied. "I've always wanted to be a performer. I'm 50, and I'm free, so it's now or never. I've got to be a star. So it costs money? So what's money?" We may still be asking, "Who is Alma Kessler?" but it's not for want of effort. Taking out an advertisement for yourself can be an expensive and sometimes humiliating experience. But you must get known—and at a certain point, as Ms. Kessler pointed out, it's "now or never."

CHAPTER 5

ON THE MOVE: INTERVIEWS, AUDITIONS, AND GETTING THE JOB

INTERVIEWS

Interviews are as much a make-or-break step on the road to getting a role as any other single act. An interview may take place through your initiative, or when a CD or producer has called *you*. In this latter (happy) case, you at least know you are in competition for a role that actually exists, even if you may be but one out of many who are called.

How important are interviews versus auditions? In Hollywood, interviews are often more important, because CDs and directors are mostly looking for what they call your "quality," which is to say your looks, personality, and personal charisma, and probably including your sex appeal. Thus, most of the competition is weeded out at the interview stage—prior to any actual auditioning. Indeed, in television and film (and sometimes even in theatre) there is often *no* audition; casting commitments are made at the interview stage (or even in the agent-producer negotiations) alone. Many veteran film actors even make it a point of personal privilege never to audition; they just meet the producer and/or director, who either is already familiar with their work or who can call up a film or two from studio vaults.

Interviews are a great stumbling block for many actors. "I don't interview well," is a common complaint, and actors capable of playing characters with strength, compassion, and subtlety fall to pieces when they are asked to play themselves.

For that's what you do in an interview: You play yourself. You must not think for a moment that an interview is simply a casual, obligatory preface to an audition. The interview is a stage on which million-dollar decisions are made, and despite the general (and desirable) state of apparent informality in which they usually take place, you are being examined very closely—and you must truly perform.

The interview is calculated to let the casting people know just what kind of person you are. Film and television directors may rely particularly on your personal quality rather than your acting: "Casting people are *afraid* of people who act," is an occasionally voiced Hollywood complaint. Because of the extremely limited rehearsal time for most television shows (and many films and plays, for that matter), producers are always partial to the actor whose own personality closely matches the characterization they want.   You must remember that they have literally *thousands* of people to choose from; so why should they take someone who's 6'3" when they are looking for someone who's 6'2"? Casting decisions are rarely that specific as to height, of course, but if you translate that into subjective qualities, you begin to see how little compromise they have to make.

How should you "perform" in an interview? Boldly. You play yourself, to be sure, but you are entitled to select *which* aspects of yourself you want to display. Be yourself, but be your *best* self. You are an actor: Look like it and act like it. You are a *professional*: Let them know that too. Arrive well ahead of time, prepared with extra copies of your photo-resume (even though you've sent one ahead), a cassette demo tape if you can, and a book of pictures of yourself. Relax and let your salable qualities shine.

Don't just sit back and wait for something to happen, however—*make it happen.* "If you were on the other side of the desk," says casting director Mike Hanks, "and you were looking for talent, what would really interest you? It's that little spark. It's really in the eye of the beholder, some little spark you see in somebody that makes them exciting, interesting, that you can identify with."[31] So ask questions. Be vivacious, not retiring. Be friendly but not self-effacing. Be funny, if you feel like it, but not at your own (or their) expense. In short, sell yourself without blasting them out of the room.

Be polite, but don't *rely* on being polite. Don't simply wait for questions and then meekly answer them; this is not a criminal investigation. Initiate questions and start the conversation yourself, when it seems possible and appropriate. You are not a butterfly mounted on a pin, a patient etherized upon a table; you have to *live* during the interview.

What will you face? You can never predict for sure: usually a casting director, perhaps a producer (maybe two or three), and maybe a secretary or another actor who happens to be in the room with you. You may be introduced to everyone; try to remember their names (and when you leave the office, write them down for future reference). Your first look when you walk in the door tells them 75% of what they wanted to know already, so make that first look a good one.   Be confident, be attractive, and show those things you consider to be your personal assets. Then sit down and get them to talk to you.

Without fail you will hear, "Well, tell me about yourself." There it is: the one big identity question that has shrivelled some actors into their own neuroses so far that they can only stammer their name, rank, and social security number. Be prepared for it. There are no rules for interviews, no forms to fill out. If you begin by telling them all your problems, the interview is over before it begins. "Well, I suppose you want to know about my credits. I don't have any." Only a psychologist can explain why so many actors destroy themselves by such remarks. Tell them about yourself—honestly, but positively, infectiously: "I want to become a working professional actor . . . I played Coriolanus at Ashland . . . I'm a short story writer for *Argosy* magazine." Of course you're insecure, but don't let it show. Don't ask, "Would it be all right if I . . . ?" It's not all right if you have to ask, so just go ahead and do it, whatever it is. Tell them things you would like them to know, and avoid things you would rather they did not know. Nobody has asked you to present both sides of the case, after all; they have every reason in the world *not* to cast you, so don't make that decision any easier for them. *Never* be desperate.

Positive personality, not repetition of facts, provides the content of the good interview. Richard Dreyfuss says of his successful first interviews, "I would try to take over . . . in the sense of going beyond those questions . . . I would *ask* questions. I would ask questions about the script, I would give them my opinion about the script. I would let them see as much of Rick Dreyfuss as possible, rather than just the information of my history."[32]

You have to be memorable, above all. CDs and producers see a great many people when casting, so you have to stand out in their memory—some way or other.   If you can look memorable, or say something memorable, or do something memorable, it helps. Mere politeness (which, after all, you must practice) is not enough to stimulate anybody's interest; *everybody* is polite. A downright hostile attitude, though not recommended, is better than stolid numbness. Be attractively unique, a bit dangerous. Find an exciting way to be different. Show them that beneath your nice exterior, and your professional calm, lies the fire of passion and charisma.

Interviewing takes practice. You should go to every interview you can, because with each you will acquire not only valuable know-how, but an unfakable confidence. It may take ten or fifteen interviews before you will really start to "come out," since the tendency of most sensitive people (and most actors *are* sensitive people) is to sit docilely and be inoffensive, just plain nice. Some of that is just nerves, face it. If you leave your interview breathing a deep sigh of relief, you've probably blown it. Conversely, if you leave feeling excited, feeling that you've met some interesting people, well then, they probably feel the same way about you, and you've probably done very well.

Here's an informative stream-of-consciousness report on the subject, from a young actor currently making headway in his career:

> Initial office report, the complexity of the office—well it's difficult to get on to it but you MUST get right on to it, right away. It's a fine line, a very fine line. You have to be up, funny, likable, charming and impressive, and yet a little bit vulnerable, and hopefully a tiny bit naive, but you can't think about *any* of that, you just have to be your own natural self, and you're being eye-balled every second—they just want to hear you talk, and that's why so many lead-off questions are "Hi, Bruce, tell me about yourself!" What could be worse? You don't know where to start. "Well, I'm a new actor, new in town, and I hope for the best . . ." No one wants to hear that, but what they want to hear is a relaxed, calm, involved person, an "on" person. But you can't be too on, too up—well, this all has to be learned. Some love it, some hate it. I love it because I'm into people and I love people and that's where you meet them—all sorts of new people—in the office.

Here's another, from a similarly successful young actor two years into a professional career:

> Perhaps the most important thing I have learned in working professionally is that "to succeed" the prime ingredient is confidence. This is not overconfidence or bravura or telling everyone what a success you're going to be. The confidence I'm talking about is an inner trust, acceptance, and knowledge of yourself. Casting directors, agents, producers, and everyone else in the business generally aren't terribly concerned about your being the next Laurence Olivier. What they are concerned with is: Are you real, responsible, confident of what you can do

and of your limitations, relaxed, dependable, and pleasant to work with and talk to, and of course whether you have the look and quality they happen to be looking for. Time and time again friends of mine have told me how they've gotten a job when they least expected it. Usually that's because they had gone to an interview or an audition not really expecting to get the part (which is not to say they were unprepared!) and were so relaxed that their natural qualities and abilities came out to their best advantage. Their attitude was *professional*, and most importantly, professional in a natural, relaxed way.

So go in there and have a good time and be yourself. And get to know the secretaries and receptionists. You need all the friends you can find.

AUDITIONS

Auditions are the means by which the stage actor and the beginning film or TV actor show what they can do. If you are at the beginning of your career, it is absolutely essential that you learn to audition, and to audition well. An audition is, of course, an artificial situation; it's a form of acting, of course, but it's not acting in a play (or a film), and it's not, in most cases, acting with other people (much less with costumes, scenery, and props). It often takes place with an audience, or an empty studio, often in the most depressing of circumstances. It is thus only a fragment of acting, and often you feel fragmented doing it.

But you *have* to do it, and you have to do it well. Young actors (and old ones, too) often have hangups about auditioning, and feel they audition much more poorly than they perform on stage or on camera. This, indeed, may be the case, but there's no use simply lamenting it. Producers with thousands of actors to choose from don't need to bother having faith in you. They will choose someone they *know* can do the role, and they will know it on the basis of that actor's audition. Even stars audition. Marlon Brando, about as big a superstar as existed at the time, auditioned for his role in *The Godfather*. Frank Sinatra auditioned for *From Here to Eternity*. Susan Sarandon auditioned for Annie in *Bull Durham*, "and let me tell you, it was humiliating," she reports.[33] For live theatre, as actress Tovah Feldshuh says, "In New York, *everybody* auditions. They may not call it that. It goes under the guise of 'going over the score,' but it's the same thing. Directors like to see who they are working with."

So, learning how to audition—and to audition well—is a necessity.

You can audition either with a prepared monologue, a prepared scene for two persons, or a cold reading, depending on the circumstances. You can also be asked to sing, to improvise, or to demonstrate specific skills.

Dramatic monologues are fairly standard for stage work, and particularly for open calls; two-person scenes are sometimes used for film and television auditions.   Stage auditions are usually in a rehearsal hall; film and TV auditions are most likely to be in a CD or producer's office (and sometimes even a home or hotel room). You must be prepared for any combination of these variables.

In *open call* auditions, you will generally be offered the opportunity to present one or two monologues, ordinarily with a two- to five-minute time limit. If there is a singing audition, sixteen bars is the usual limit; the call will usually state if you are to sing *a cappella*, or bring an accompanist, or whether an accompanist will be provided (in which case you bring your sheet music). Sometimes you can bring your own accompaniment via a prerecorded cassette tape and cassette player; in this case, you should have it *precisely cued up* (allowing time to turn it on, put it down, and start singing), and you should *practice singing with it* many times before the actual audition.

Open call auditions are the "cattle calls" of show business; CDs may see twenty or thirty of you an hour (many more if it's a dance audition), and it's hard not to get depressed at the minimal attention you'll be getting, and the massive competition for that minimal attention. If you've seen *A Chorus Line*, you know what it's all about. That show was created by people who knew professional auditions from the inside out. Still, people do get cast from open calls, and persistence pays off. A UCLA master's student, Jim Birge, monitored 16,086 Equity Principal (now Eligible Performer) auditions in 1981; these resulted in 155 actual work contracts, which is to say that almost 1% of those auditioning got cast. Elinore O'Connell, newly in Equity at the time of the auditions for the Los Angeles *Les Misérables* company, simply *knew* that Fantine was her role. She prepared her audition daily for months before the open call. But 3,000 actors showed up at the appointed date, and she didn't make it in the room on either of the first two days. On the third and final day of auditions, O'Connell arrived at the theatre before dawn, but found that hundreds of actors had camped out all night; she still couldn't get in. Undaunted, she asked if she could wait at the door anyway, in the hopes that someone wouldn't show up; well, everybody showed up, but a production assistant finally had some pity on her—and as the sun set over the Hollywood Hills, O'Connell was asked to come on in and sing. Yes, of course, she got the role.

Every actor should have prepared audition pieces always at the ready. You never know when you might get a chance to audition, and you should have a few pieces ready to go without thinking much about it. Often you will do a couple of prepared pieces not quite in the range of the parts being cast (how are you supposed to know?) and the director will ask "Got anything else?" or "Have anything funny?" Obviously, you should be ready to oblige.

For stage work your audition pieces should be monologues. Most LORT auditions ask for two contrasting monologues, one in verse and one in prose, delivered in no more than four minutes. Usually, one of these pieces should be something written before the nineteenth century, and one should be fairly contemporary. Graduate auditions through U/RTA should be in this format, also. Although it is rarely required that one monologue be from a comedy, it is usually quite helpful if one is—casting directors who may hear dozens of monologues in a three-hour casting session are ordinarily quite grateful for something that is genuinely funny, witty, or charming—among all the Medeas and Hamlets.

For film and television general auditions you should prepare scenes with a partner rather than monologues, and with a partner who will generally be available for fast-breaking opportunities that may arrive in the future. Choose your scenes and rehearse them carefully.

In preparing auditions, you should keep the following in mind:

- *Brevity* is essential. If four minutes is specified as a maximum, that doesn't mean that three minutes and fifty-nine seconds is the minimum. Don't try to fill up the time frame; give yourself some elbow room, and deliver a real jolt: theatrical *impact*. Your audition should grab the CD's attention right away, tease and taunt a bit, build to a climax, and then end powerfully.

- The *grabber* is critically important: You might not be aware of it, but directors generally get hooked in the first few seconds—or not at all. They want to get dazzled, and dazzled fast. Remember, the casting people are not passive and objective educators, looking for flaws and readying academic "critiques"; they are producers, looking for someone who will capture an audience, entertain them, wring them out, and send them home—raving about the show to their friends. You have four minutes to prove to them that that's you.

- The prepared monologue or scene should show you in a role in which you could be cast *today*. Particularly if you are auditioning for a film or television role, do something very close to your age and personality, and something in a style as close as possible to the style of the part for which you are auditioning. If you are auditioning at a dinner theatre, it is silly to do a scene from *Othello*. Even if you played old ladies in college, you will not do them on Broadway, so don't give them your Aunt Eller until you are in your fifties.

- Choose audition material that is self-explanatory. In no case should you explain, before your audition, the plot of the scene or the characterization you are trying to convey. At most you should say the name of the scene and proceed. Choose scenes that don't require specific pieces of furniture, properties, or extensive movement—scenes you could present in a variety of locations and without bringing a suitcase full of production aids.

- Choose audition material that is not shopworn; stay away from monologue books, and try to find fresh material. This isn't always easy, of course, for what is fresh to some is old hat to another. For example:

OMAR PAXSON: I get tired hearing the same thing over and over. [Find] a couple of minor characters from Shakespeare that no one ever does, like Launce and Crab from *Two Gentlemen of Verona*. I never hear that.

ERIC CHRISTMAS: There is a list of pieces that you hear so often you wish they wouldn't do them. For example, Launce and his dog Crab turns up all the time.

These contradictory words of advice, moreover, are from the same audition textbook! It's no surprise, however; what is old hat in one year, or place, is a novelty in other quarters.

- It is frequently rewarding to find and extract scenes from contemporary *novels* for audition material; chances are the dialogue is realistic and the scene fresh. Remember, they are judging *you*, not the material, and it doesn't have to be a masterpiece for them to like you doing it.

- Choose audition material that is *exciting*, that excites you and the people you can get to look at it. "What good is truth if it's dull and boring?" says Michael Shurtleff in his excellent book, *Audition*.[34]

- Go *all the way*, emotionally, with your audition. There's no sense in holding back, waiting for a director to show you the way; unless you're cast, there will be no director. Don't over-estimate how much CDs can see into your silences and private reveries; let your feelings and words come out where they can be seen, heard, and *felt*. Excite the listeners. "How strong should the reading be?" asks "Dynasty" CD Gary Shaffer. "The exciting readings get the role," he answers. "From my experience, the closer you get to performance level in your reading, the better chance you have of getting cast. The person who cries real tears gets the job."[35]

- *Preparedness* is, of course, critical. How much should you prepare? There is no easy answer to that question; you can be overrehearsed, but you can never be overprepared. Preparation is what gives you confidence and calm—it takes your mind off yourself and lets you concentrate on the business at hand. A relaxed preparedness is perhaps the most professional attitude you can bring to an audition. When George C. Scott first decided he wanted to become an actor, he decided to read for the leading part in a campus production. Getting a copy of the script, he memorized the *entire part*, word for word, before he had the audition. "They were flabbergasted, nobody had ever bothered to learn the part for an audition. I got the role." All too frequently actors refuse to prepare on the grounds that it will rob them of spontaneity, but it takes little objective contemplation to realize that spontaneity is the result of careful, not shoddy preparation. And that sort of preparation is never wasted.

- Prepare your scenes under the *various circumstances* in which you may have to perform them. Rehearse on large stages and in small, officelike rooms. Rehearse with a "director" watching you, or try out your audition piece as often as you can in an acting class, at a party, in your home, or wherever you can get an audience of one or more to see you. Get used to performing amidst general inattention and extraneous noise. Rehearse and prepare your introduction to your scene, your transition between one monologue and the next, and even the "thank you" with which you conclude your audition. Obvious unpreparedness is instant death in a prepared-scene audition, for if you have not taken the time and energy to work on your audition, how can you demonstrate your willingness to expend time and energy on your part?

- Keep your scenes *loose*, and not dependent on any single planned "effect." Let the environment of your performance, whether it be office or stage, affect what you and your partner do. Preparation does not necessarily mean rehearsing and fixing every movement and gesture of a scene; some actors prefer to prepare the lines of a scene only, and leave the physical and emotional actions free and unrehearsed. This is particularly useful for film and television auditions, and in fact more closely duplicates the way these scenes would be shot professionally than conventional stage rehearsing would. Remember, in an audition the producer is not looking for a completed performance, but for your ability to act convincingly (and, when you have a partner, to *react* convincingly, as well).

- Choose for your acting partner someone you trust completely. He or she should be willing to give you the focus if it is your audition. You might respond by working up some scenes your partner can use for auditions. But no matter whose scene it is, you look better if your partner is good rather than bad, so never select a poor partner in the hope of looking good by comparison.

- If you are permitted, or required, to do two scenes, choose two that differ in tone and style rather than in age. Generally you are asked to do contrasting scenes, such as comedy and drama, or (particularly with stage work) classical and modern. Do not think of these categories as absolute, and do not worry too much about whether *Tartuffe* is funny or serious or whether *St. Joan* is modern or classical. The point is to get two differing scenes that show you off to your best advantage. If you are confused about what kinds of scenes they want, ask.

- Above all, choose material that shows you at your best. You don't want your audition scenes to be merely good; you want them to be *great*; you want them to be *terrific*. Choose material at which you excel, even if it means not doing exactly what they have asked for or what has been suggested here. The audition fails if you do not come off looking better than anybody they have seen that day, and a merely competent job with material you don't like is as bad as nothing at all. Have your agent, if you have one, preview your audition pieces and comment. If you are doing a full stage audition, by all means get a director to help you.

- In actually giving your prepared audition, *take the stage*. Take and claim your space. You may know from experience that you're likely to be interrupted sixteen bars into your song, or fifteen seconds into your monologue, but put that out of your mind. For those fifteen seconds or five minutes, dominate the stage you are on and make it your own, for if you don't trust yourself, why should they? Make it a great sixteen bars, a terrific fifteen seconds. Never look as though you're waiting to be cut off; want to go on, and on, and on!

- Can you use a prop? A simple but appropriate prop that you can keep in your pocket, and bring out at precisely the right moment, can humanize and give a lift to an audition, particularly in a modern piece. One actor reports losing a role in call-backs because of a very cleverly incorporated flash instamatic camera in his competitor's audition; "a brilliant and outrageous idea," our colleague reports, "but I was edged out by a *camera*!" Now you, too, can do some edging out.

- Don't look directly at the auditioners unless they ask you to, but direct your audition generally toward them, a little to the side or over their heads. Let them see you as fully as possible. Choose the characters you're speaking to, and "place" them out in the audience, not to your profile.

- In group auditions, where other actors are waiting their turn, you may find you have a tendency to play to your fellow actors in the wings, rather than to the producers out front. This is easy to understand, for although the other actors may be your competition, they are also your peers, and you may find them a more comfortable audience. Don't. This is the time to turn your back on the competition, as it were, and take the stage as your own. Cruel? No. You are not auditioning as part of an ensemble, but as an individual actor. They will be, too.

- *Dress* for the audition. It is not necessary, and in fact it is sometimes downright harmful, to costume yourself fully for the part you're reading for, at least during your first audition. But it is vitally important to *look the part*, drawing on clothing from your own wardrobe, or clothing that *could* be in your own wardrobe. If it's a western, by all means dig out your Arizona gear; if it's in a law office, grab your pinstriped suit. Don't go so far as to look silly on the street, and don't go all the way into period dress—it may make you feel uncomfortable, and will almost certainly make you look desperate. Look the part without looking like you're trying to look the part. Look like you *are* the part.

- And *look* like a professional actor. That does not mean to look like a college actor. As a rule, college actors are poorer and dress in a more slovenly way than professional actors. This may be fine in college, but it doesn't cut the same figure off the campus. Let's face it: Professional CDs, producers, and directors make good incomes, have American Express cards, stay in good hotels, eat in good restaurants, and associate mainly with *employed* actors. They may be artists, but they are also adult businesspersons in a grown-up world. Regardless of what we might think of the artistic temperament, the lifestyle of most regional theatre directors (and for that matter New York and Hollywood casting directors) is fairly conservative, and fairly middle class. Ripped jeans, bare feet, and stained T-shirts just don't have the same effect at AEA studios, in Hollywood or New York offices, or on resident theatre stages that they do in the state university experimental theatre. You, of course, have every right to be yourself and dress as you choose, and people will rarely *think* they are judging you on the basis of your clothing (much less admit as much) but to "dress down" for an audition (even if you simply cannot afford to dress "up") can create a level of alienation that your audition may not overcome. The image of disaffected youth is not one that you want to project in a professional audition. Even if you seek to become the long awaited "next James Dean," you had better learn to be comfortable in adult attire. Actors and actresses are not looked down upon in the least for auditioning in fashionable dresses, handsome jackets, trendy sweaters, shined shoes, managed hairstyles, and sharp, contemporary outfits. These are not at all *necessary*, and they won't—by themselves—get you any roles, but they will lead you to a quicker and higher degree of rapport with people who, after all, dress more or less the same way.

- One final word on clothes: You must be completely *comfortable* in them. If you are only comfortable in tattered campus gear, then that's what you're going to have to wear, until and unless you get accustomed to something better. You can't worry about the way you look. Worry, of course, is murder.

- Get in the light. Stay in the light. Speak up and be heard.

- When you finish your audition, don't apologize for anything. Don't give any indication that you aren't proud of what you did. This is not a time for abject humility (nor, on the other hand, for cocky smugness); if it seems appropriate, you might ask if there's anything else the auditioners might want to hear. You should do everything in your power at this point to convince your audience that you love to audition, that you enjoyed doing this audition particularly, and that you'd be happy to do it again if they were interested. Confidence, after all, is part of what you're being auditioned for; your auditors are looking not only for talent and what is appropriate, but for personal stamina and a positive, profes- sional attitude. Don't turn them off by grimaces or mutter- ings that convey your personal discomfort, and only show that you're not yet ready for professional work.

- Auditions and interviews are both *competitions,* and you must understand and treat them as such. You are being examined for your usefulness in an industry that wants to make money through your efforts. There are many competitors for every acting job; each, in effect, is put on a moving treadmill and passed in front of the casting directors and producers. It is your task to *stop the treadmill* and make the auditioners take notice of your individual value to their project. Whatever you can do to accomplish that, within the bounds of your own ability and—yes—ethics, you ought to know how to do, and be prepared to do.

COLD READINGS

Prepared scenes are for general audition purposes; cold readings are for a specific job.

In a cold reading you are given a copy of a script, often a typed manuscript, and often only a "side," which is a portion of the text with just your lines and their immediate cues. You are then asked to read aloud for the producers, often with other actors reading the other parts. Or, you may read with a stage manager or with the director or producer. In a cold reading, you are going for a specific part, so you know that a part at least exists, and you haven't yet been ruled out for it. So, you're getting closer! If you are right for the role, you may just get it. Your goal is to be *terrific*.

There can be several rounds of cold readings: an initial one followed by any number of call-backs. After a certain point, union actors can get paid for call-back readings.

Your cold reading should be delivered just like your prepared auditions: powerfully, professionally, and confidently. It should also be true to the text as written. As Broadway director Hal Prince (*Phantom of the Opera*) suggests, "The people who audition well come out, stand still, read the lines as they appear on paper—they don't ad lib changes, they don't improvise, they don't swallow their lines into their sleeves because they object to being there in the first place. I don't know of another way of getting a job in the theatre."[36]

A cold reading need not be entirely cold, and if the idea of cold readings frightens you (and it should), there is plenty you can do about it. Ordinarily you can read the script beforehand, perhaps in the office waiting room. Arrive early. SAG contracts also provide that you can get the script at least twenty-four hours before—although this is, quite frankly, not always possible in television, where scripts are under constant rewrite. But even if the script is thrust into your hands at the moment you're asked to read, you will probably have the chance to skim through the text if you ask for it, and you should. You can ask a question, too, such as "Is this guy a wimp?" or "Do I really fall in love with him?"   You might be shy of asking, but most directors and producers are happy to talk for a minute or two about what they want, given the chance. Don't ask multiple questions, or seek to initiate any lengthy discussion, but you certainly should know the character's basic age, social standing, and specific goals in the scene before tearing off into your reading. Try to phrase just the right *specific* question (not "What do you want here?"), and then let the director help you out.

Don't worry if you can't pronounce certain words or if you muff odd lines. Nobody expects a polished performance at a cold reading, and no directors (no good directors, anyway) care at this point for absolute perfection of detail. What they are looking for is the essential character, and your basic theatricality in the role. Do you understand the part? Will you? Will you be sympathetic? Will you be exciting? Sexy? Entertaining? Will your presence *improve* the part, flesh it out, from what lies there silently on the page? Are you going to be fun to work with?

If you excite them with your reading, and they feel you can learn what you have to learn between now and dress rehearsal, or the first take, you're in the running. If, on the other hand, you get flustered because you mispronounce the name of a foreign city or a character's name, your preoccupation with this lapse will ruin your reading, even though you may be the only one who noticed.

Your auditors are looking for *acting* skills, not reading facility. So *get your eyes off the page as much as you can.* Don't be misled by the term "reading"; the less you have to look at your script, the less you actually "read" it, the better you will be able to approach performance level, and a performance is, after all, what they're ultimately going to want from you. One useful trick is to keep your finger on the script at the proper place, and to "spot-memorize" a phrase or sentence at a time, so you can deliver your words while looking at the (real or imaginary) character you are addressing. Then, when you are ready to turn back to the text, your finger will point you to the next line to spot-memorize. In any event, never get buried in the pages before you. They want to see your eyes, they *want to see you see.* They want to see *what you see.* Always remember that you are demonstrating your ability to act, not to read.

If you can keep (or otherwise acquire) a copy of the script, do so, then memorize the part for any call-backs.

Intensity, persuasiveness, sexual longing, passion, madcap inventiveness—these are wonderful qualities to show in a cold reading, where they are appropriate to the material (and only you can judge what's appropriate), and maybe even where they are *not* appropriate. Blandness and passivity are the only true crimes in this medium. But it is best to avoid any broad external characterization in a cold reading, unless you are certain that this is what is absolutely demanded by the part and the producer, and unless you can do broad external characterizations extremely well. Read the character as yourself—as your most intense, exciting self—to the greatest extent possible, and let the director see your basic personal qualities and idiosyncrasies through your acting. If the role requires a dialect and you can do it perfectly, do it; if you can only fake it, don't try. In general, don't try *anything* in a professional audition that will make you look less than wonderful, unless they ask you to.

The reading will end when the casting director has ruled you in or out: "in" meaning "in at least through the next round of call-backs." Often, however, a director will be ambivalent or uncertain. You aren't exactly asked to leave, but you can tell that the director isn't entirely satisfied; no decision has been made yet. This is a good time to ask, "Excuse me, but do you think in this scene Martha should be a little sexier?" (Or "bitchier?" or "more compassionate?" or "funnier?") You might get a chance to do it again, and in a manner closer to the director's concept. If you get coaching, put it to use. This is not the time to debate or disagree, but to deliver!

You can work on your cold reading technique, of course, in the privacy of your home or in specialized classes. Tony Barr, CBS producer and head of the Film Actors' Workshop, advises that "You should work your tail off learning to become a good cold reader. Your career will probably hinge on it. Take a speed reading course. At the very least, read aloud from any source whatsoever for at least fifteen minutes a day, taking your eyes off the page as much as you can without interrupting the flow of your reading."

Sometimes in an audition or an interview you will be asked to take off your clothes. Contemporary films frequently involve nudity, and so, from time to time, does contemporary theatre. There are strict union regulations regarding this, and you should be aware of them. It is entirely proper for a director to get some idea of what your body looks like, and you might be asked to show your shape without having to undress. Under no circumstances, however, may a director ask you to undress without having informed you *when the appointment was made* that the part involves nudity and that you will be asked to disrobe during the audition. This at least gives you time to check out the producer and make sure you know what you are getting into. Union rules also require that you may bring a *friend* to the audition in these cases. Remember that your agent and the union (even if you are not a member) will protect you from unscrupulous voyeurs who happen to be producing films and plays. On the other hand, if you plan to do nude films or plays, you had better plan on doing nude auditions as well.

You will have to adopt a pretty stable audition attitude. Like everything else in the life of a beginning professional actor, auditions can lead to paranoia. Even if everybody from the producer on down is extremely polite, you are nevertheless unceremoniously directed to perform when they ask you and to leave when they tell you. Frequently you are ushered onto a stage and see nothing in front of you but bright lights and a few shadowy forms at the back, and you hear nothing but "Name!" "Well, let's see it!" and, in the middle of your prepared monologue, "Thank you very much. Next please!" It is discouraging to the strong and ruinous to the weak, and you had better be prepared for it. A professional attitude is your point of strength. Remember always that you have to stop the audition treadmill. Only if you are solidly confident can you be strong enough to do that.

THE SCREEN TEST

Screen tests are still sometimes used in Hollywood to see how you look on camera. The screen test may be a very simple affair whereby you turn your face from left to right in front of a camera and speak some lines or improvise a conversation. Or it can be as involved as a complete scene that you rehearse with a studio director and perform with sets and costumes. For major roles in films and television series, the screen test is usually the last stage of the audition, and the finalists for a certain role may screen-test opposite each other. Only newcomers are ordinarily screen-tested, however, since veteran actors can be seen by studio executives in actual film or taped performances available to them on call.

Screen tests are not as common as they once were; on the other hand, videotaping of auditions has become routine, especially in Hollywood, and it is virtually universal in commercial casting. It has even become common for stage auditions. Videotape allows a director to hang onto your audition for a while, to show it to other people after you've left the office, and to examine you closely and repeatedly against other contenders for the same role. It is wise to study camera-acting, and to work with videotaping equipment, as preparation for your career. There are numerous commercial schools, advertising regularly in the trades, that offer both instruction and facilities for taping auditions and scenes, and you should explore these opportunities.

NONDRAMATIC OPTIONS

So far we have been considering primarily dramatic options: plays, films, and television shows. Before going further, it would be wise to give some special consideration to three other options: commercials, industrials, and "extra" work.

Commercials

Commercials form a staple income for many actors between their dramatic roles, and some actors make their careers solely in commercial acting. The top pay, as you probably already know, is outstanding when it comes: Actors typically make from $5,000 to $20,000 or more from a day's work on a nationally broadcast commercial. SAG actors, in fact, earn considerably more from acting in commercials than from TV or films. In 1988 SAG performers picked up $344.5 million in commercials, against only $309 million in television shows, and $187 million in films.

Commercials are cast and produced in both New York and Los Angeles, and sometimes in other cities as well. New York leads L.A. by an increasing margin in this field. About two-thirds of all national TV commercials are produced in New York, with a quarter in L.A. and about a tenth in Chicago (the up-and-coming "third city"). Specialized agencies handle most of the casting and production for this mini-art form.

Rounds, interviews, and auditions for commercial work follow pretty much the same pattern as their counterparts in film and television work, except there is more of everything—more rounds, more interviews, more photos, and more pavement pounding. Commercial actors are always "on the street," often with garment bags in their back seat or over their shoulder, for the work is rarely more than a day at a time, and there's tremendous competition for each little part. A union card is essential for commercial work, but you can get on the street without one, armed with a *Ross Reports* (in New York) or with one of several studio guides in Los Angeles.

Commercials don't always use all of you. There are specialists in this field—"hand" people, for example, who are never seen but from the wrist outward, usually holding the product in a provocative manner. Honey-tongued speakers can "audition" by making *audio* demo tapes for voice-overs; these are the voices that speak off-camera, narrating or bringing home the message of the commercial. Many professional studios will make such demos for you (they advertise in the trades), and agencies will listen to them. "The most successful people in business," says one commercial producer, "knock on doors and send tapes. They apply themselves. With talent and application you've got to make it in this town (Los Angeles) because this town soaks up talent."[37]

Virtually everyone admits that acting in commercials "is not acting." In fact, some of it is deliberately "bad" acting, by normal standards, so as to "burn in" (an advertising term) the sponsor's message all the more forcefully. "Ring around the collar! Ring around the collar!" You might feel better about it if you considered acting in commercials as acting in a 30-second Bertolt Brecht "theatre of alienation" play, where your goal is not to create a convincing character, but to convey an idea (OK, to sell a product) to the audience. It's an alienating role, that's for sure. "We have no names," laments one commercial actor, "we're just the 'talent.' 'Send the talent out!' they call. They never even ask your names." "It's demeaning," says Linda Kelsey (a commercial actress who has graduated to starring roles in prime-time TV), "it's kind of plastic acting—instead of selling the truth of a character you're playing, you sell the fantasy of the product." But it is lucrative work, it is honest work, and you meet a lot of people on their way up too; today's commercial director is very likely tomorrow's film director. Commercials also get your face on the screen, often in L.A. and New York, where it counts. Sandy Duncan's professional career took off with a California bank commercial, which, although shown only locally, gave her great visibility in Los Angeles; without that commercial she wouldn't have played Peter Pan in Peoria. And Mariette Hartley's career accelerated after her Polaroid ads; this sort of thing will probably be happening more, not less, in the future.

If you go for commercial work, go for it fully, and respect the work for what it is. "Never, for a minute, feel superior to it or treat it with disdain," writes Cortland Jessup. "Don't waste your time passing judgments or getting caught up in the 'is it acting or not' debate."[38]

Commercial work requires bright spontaneity, strong discipline, and improvisational skills (much of Hartley's work in the Polaroid commercials came out of her own in-studio improvisation). "I use the same technique to learn a 60-second spot as [to do] Neil Simon," says Beverly Sanders, one of the finest performers in the field. "The key to me in commercials is to listen. You must be a quick study, and you must pay attention to the director, to *everyone*. It really takes a good actor to do a good job."[39] It took Sanders eighteen months of foot pounding to get her first commercial, but now she has done hundreds of them and has made it her career. You may wish to try it only part-time, if at all. If you do, go into it with a full commitment.

There are many classes in both New York and Hollywood–Los Angeles on commercial acting technique (they advertise in the trades), and there are also a couple of worthwhile books on the subject listed in the appendix.

Business Theatre: Industrial Shows

Business theatre consists of productions mounted by corporations or industries (they are often called "industrial shows"), which are, more or less, the "commercials" of live theatre—though a great deal less frequent. Over a hundred producers across the country produce these shows, which are presented at dealers' conventions, buyers' conventions, and other in-house gatherings of corporations or national groups of various kinds. The industrial show can be based around a theme, or used to introduce a new product, or even to sing the praises of the corporation's management and history. Many of these shows are splashy mini-epics, produced with great professional skill, and on high budgets.

Performing in industrials usually demands first-class musical skills (singing and dancing); good stage credits are also highly desirable if not mandatory. The pay is excellent (it's Equity's highest minimum salary), the working conditions sometimes spectacular (you may perform in the Caribbean or Hawaii), and the duration is short, putting you back on the street before you know it, a little tanner and a lot richer. Almost all business theatre is packaged in New York; you can get the names of producers from the occasional listings in *Show Business* (the New York trade paper). The days of business theatre may be waning, however, and in 1988 actor work weeks (1,771) in industrial productions were only a third of what they were two decades before.

Business theatre income accounted for only 1 1/2% of Equity actor earnings in 1988, so you shouldn't be planning a career around this alternative lifestyle.

Working as an "Extra"

Working as a film extra may also pay some of your bills until the big day arrives, and it could also get you into the Screen Extras Guild (SEG). What's important about that? Only that three days of SEG work can "sister" you into SAG, and six days or so can make you an Eligible Performer for Equity stage auditions.

As a film extra, you may, if you wish, "Taft-Hartley"—that is, you may work for up to thirty consecutive days *without* joining the union—but after that time you must join SEG (current initiation fee: $600). In return you will make $91 per day for standing around while the cameras roll, $101 if they need your "special ability" in the scene, and $145 if you are asked to do a "silent bit." Plus, you get an extra $20 if you get cold or wet—and additional salary emollients for like indignities. Don't expect to get discovered by being an extra—it almost never happens—and don't expect to get rich. Of the more than 5,000 SEG members, only a handful of pluggers make $25,000 a year. Most SEG members are earning pin money, and seeking to brighten up their otherwise quite comfortable lives. It *is* a chance for you to hang around a movie set while the work is going on, however, picking up pointers and possibly meeting people in the process.

You can sign up to be seen for extra work in L.A. at the famous Central Casting Office at 2600 West Olive Street (5th floor), in Burbank, CA 91505 (telephone [818] 596–5200). New non-union clients can register here on Monday, Wednesday, and Friday, from 2:00 to 4:00 P.M. Call first, and plan to bring your driver's license and a photo (a 3 x 5 color photo is OK here)—there is currently a $5.00 fee. Be prepared to wait: Central Casting already has 4,000 clients. You can also call Central Casting to find out what they're hiring this week: men should call (818) 569–5145; women call (818) 569–5811. There are a number of other extra casting agencies in L.A. as well; check down the road at D.I.S.C. Casting at 3601 W. Olive Avenue #800 in Burbank (telephone [818] 955–6000). D.I.S.C.'s recorded casting information is available for men at [818] 841–7644 and for women at [818] 841–3744. A number of extra casting services are also active in New York City; you can check with Hyde-Hamlet Casting in the Actors' Equity Building (165 West 46th Street, #1115, NY 10036 [212] 730-1842) or Todd Thaler Casting (130 West 57th Street, NY 10019 [212] 246-7116); both these services look at non-union as well as union talent. Updated addresses and phone numbers for these and other extra casting offices may be found in *Extra Casting Agencies*, an occasional booklet you can usually find at the Universal News Agency at 1655 Las Palmas in Hollywood (just south of Hollywood Blvd.) and at some theatre book shops.

THE JOB OFFER

If you have played all your cards right, if you are as good as you think you are, and if your contacts, interviews, auditions, and cold readings have gone well, you may be offered a part. You now have to decide whether you will take it or not. For most actors, this is the easiest decision of their lives.

There are some jobs, however, that you might want to think twice about taking, even if they are the first thing that comes your way.

The job could be a nonunion job. Many theatres and independent film companies skirt union regulations and jurisdiction. Even though they may pay you a union scale wage, they do not operate according to certain procedures that the union requires of all producers. Check with the union. If the producer is operating in frank violation of union regulations, you may find yourself blackballed from future employment. This is rare, but investigate. If it happens to you, you may never live it down.

The job could be quasi-union. That is, it could be a workshop or experimental production (student films come under this category) that operates under a special waiver or dispensation from the union. In such a case you may not be paid, or you may be given "deferred payment," which means you will not get the money until the project is successfully marketed. If the project is nonunion but operated in accordance with the union, you have nothing to fear from participation, but you might not get more out of it than the work itself.

The job could be union but far from the city (*any* city), keeping you from auditioning for bigger things in the near future. You could be hired, for example, at a summertime Equity dinner theatre in the mountains, and while you're carrying spears and waiting on tourists, you're also missing auditions for the next Broadway and off-Broadway season in New York.

The job could be a porno film. These come in two categories. The independent nonunion X-rated films (and stage equivalents) are utterly useless to you except as a source of income, and the income is pretty low. The days are over when actors or actresses could have their careers ruined for posing or performing in the nude—but we have not reached the point where their careers will particularly be helped by it either.

Then there are "serious" nude films, or at least serious films (or plays) that have nude or seminude sequences. You shouldn't be surprised if you're asked to go along; mainline Broadway hits such as *Equus, Amadeus, Hurlyburly*—together with most important "R" rated films—include topless and/or bottomless sequences for women, and sometimes frontal nudity for men. You may say that you will only do such a scene if it is "tastefully done"—but, naturally, everyone will assure you that "*of course*, it will be tastefully done," and the real problem is there is no way to tell what they mean by "tasteful" until the final cut or dress rehearsal. So you will simply have no idea when you take the role just what parts of you your mother will see when she goes to see you in it. At any rate, don't hold out hope that "if they want me badly enough, they'll get a double for the nude scenes." They probably won't want you that badly.

And doing nude scenes may be even harder than you think, even in films (where you might think you only have to do it once.) If it were a matter of simply flipping off a robe, shooting a quick scene, and then dressing again, that would be one thing. More often, even for a simple 10-second shot, many hours of takes and retakes will be required. Yes, SAG rules require a closed set in such cases, but you still will find yourself standing, sitting, and lying around in the nude amidst fifty technicians, actors, and producers (all fully dressed, of course) while they take, focus, retake, and refocus your 10-second nude scene, taking coffee breaks in between. Strong, uninhibited actresses have been reduced to quivering tears by this dehumanizing process, which, after all, is exactly how the Nazis humiliated prisoners. Tovah Feldshuh turned down half a million dollars to star in the film *Exquisite Beauty*, finding that she was to be in the nude for forty pages of script; there are some things that money cannot and should not buy, and you might want to consider your own stamina for this kind of thing.

The role may be otherwise offensive. It may be pornographic, or the style of the material may be too clichéd and ridiculous for your taste and talent. You may be asked to work with actors or directors you do not respect, or in a television show you loathe. You may be asked to do a commercial for a product you find personally disgusting, or to do a dialect you find ethnically or racially degrading. The role, you may feel, may be too small.

There are, then, a number of possible reasons why you might not choose to accept every job that comes your way, and why you might want to wait until the "right one" comes along. For every acceptance ties you up and holds you back from possibilities not yet known. But this is mainly cavil, isn't it? Lucille Ball once said that the way she got to the top of her profession was by taking *absolutely every job* she could get. Tony Curtis was quoted in *Variety*, as saying, "I think anybody in this business should take any job he can get today." Jason Robards says, "The only advice I have for young people is, no matter how you do it, do it in front of people who pay."[40] So unless you sense an utter and absolute catastrophe ahead, TAKE THE JOB. There is more than just an immediate reason for this: One job will lead to another, power begets power. One fine actor worked steadily for ten years, at which time he looked back and realized that *every single job* he had gotten (except the first) evolved out of a previous one. A beginning actor, therefore, should refuse a paying acting job only for extraordinarily compelling reasons.

HOW MUCH WILL YOU MAKE?

You have a job. Now that you have struggled, humbled yourself, and suffered financial hardships by the carload, you are ready to cash in your chips, right? What will the job pay?

As we've made clear so far, the income of an actor is not great. But if you work you get paid, and you should know how much that will be.

All the unions have negotiated contracts on your behalf; these contracts specify, among other things, the minimum salaries you will receive. These salary "scales" are written in astonishing detail; the Codified Basic Agreement negotiated between the Screen Actors Guild and the various motion picture producers is a 172-page book. The contracts are renegotiated continuously upon expiration, so the following information, which is accurate as of this printing, is subject to regular change.

Stage Roles

If you land a part in a Broadway play, or in the national tour of a Broadway play, you are covered by Equity's Production Contract.

Your minimum weekly salary will be $775 in 1989, although at some "endangered" Broadway theatres the scale can be somewhat lower, down to $620, per a concession from the union. Your touring expenses for a road show are, of course, completely covered as well, including your housing and meal expenses, and a little spending money. Under the Production Contract in 1987–1988, 47,446 actor work weeks were registered and $52.3 million earned; that's about 22% of the work, and 41.5% of the income, for stage actors.

The off-Broadway contract minimum depends on two factors: the size of the theatre (its number of seats) and the actual weekly gross for the production. You won't know, therefore, until the show is running. The range is from $280 to $530, with several dozen stops in between. A "hit" off-Broadway show will bring you at least $505, even at the smallest such theatre. American actors in 1987–1988 earned about $4.8 million off-Broadway.

If you are cast in a resident theatre on the LORT circuit, your salary minimum is determined by the size of the theatre's potential gross ticket sales. The largest (A) theatres paid a minimum 1989 salary of $477 per week. B+ theatres pay $465; B theatres, $454; C theatres, $431; and D theatres (the smallest), $364. You can ascertain a theatre's rating size through the current *Theatre Profiles*. In 1987–1988, Equity members notched up 63,123 LORT work weeks, Equity's highest number of weeks, but only $28.7 million in earnings, hardly half the earnings under the Production Contract. However, sometimes housing is also provided in LORT contracts, along with other local perks.

CORST and COST theatres—stock companies—are also rated by the size of their operations. CORST is divided into three classes, X, Y, and Z, with a range from $441.06 (X) to $369.42 (Z). COST has two categories: "small" companies pay a minimum of $408.81; "large" pay $448.88. Stock companies produced 6% of actor income in 1987–1988.

The SPT (Small Professional Theatre) Contract, newly developed for smaller-than-LORT resident professional enterprises, has salaries of $100–$390. Equity reported 16,710 work weeks under this contract in 1987–1988, at places like the American Stage Company in St. Petersburg, the Portland Repertory Theatre, and the Stage Guild of Washington, D.C. And the LOA (Letter of Agreement) contract, at similar rates, was used for about 18,000 work weeks the same year; together these developing theatres produced 5.5% of actor income in 1987–1988.

The highest salary minimum? That's for employment in industrial shows. You will get $931 minimum for a week's work there, although the minimum drops to $775 if you're hired for two weeks or more.

These are minimum salaries, of course; you can get more, but you probably won't get *much* more. So that you know what's out there, the 1988 *average* weekly salaries under each of these contracts—averaging out stars, veterans, and newcomers alike—were, in descending order:

Production (Broadway and national Broadway tours): $1,104

Industrials: $1,075

Stock (CORST and COST): $649

LORT: $455

Dinner Theatre: $441

Off-Broadway: $394

CAT (Chicago Area Theatres): $380

Developing Theatres (SPT and LOA): $203

Want to drop lower? The 99-seat theatre production code in Los Angeles currently requires a "salary" of $5 to $14 per performance (whether you need it or not?) and, at the time of writing, the L.A. theatre producers are fighting the code's establishment, saying that it will bankrupt their operations. And maybe it will.

If you are hired as a paid *apprentice*, you are not covered by any union contract, so your salary or stipend is more or less at the caprice of management. Fifty or $100 a week was a fairly standard non-Equity apprentice stipend in 1989. If you are hired for a nonunion outdoor drama, your salary might vary from around $100 to over $400, with $150 above average; rehearsal salaries are apt to be a bit less. Many of these theatres offer low-cost, company-arranged housing and other incentives as well, however. Shakespeare festivals pay a season stipend of anywhere from a few hundred dollars to $1,500 or more, plus housing, for up to fourteen weeks of rehearsals and performances.

Very few actors live on stage earnings alone. "The situation for an actor in New York these days is that one can't afford to be an actor," says Paul Hecht, who won a Tony nomination for his role in *Rosencranz and Guildenstern Are Dead* in 1967, and in 1988–1989 starred (to extravagant praise) as Enrico IV at the off-Broadway Roundabout Theatre, and as Menenius in the New York Shakespeare Festival production of *Coriolanus*. "I get calls all the time to do plays—for $227 a week!" Hecht reports, adding that for Enrico and Menenius he received only "$500 and change [weekly], of which you pay 10% to an agent and 2% to your union—and then how much to the government? I don't even know what other job it's comparable to. And we're talking about people who are high up in their profession, not people just out of school. You're looking at a middle-aged man at the height of his artistic powers who has to treat these experiences as if they were artistic sabbaticals. But I'm an actor, and I love the theatre, and I'm stuck."[41] Hecht makes his living doing voice-over commercials. "Every actor that you see on the stage in New York and America today who is not in a Broadway play is underwriting the American theatre," Hecht concludes.

Film/TV

If you find employment in films or television shows, higher minimums prevail. Basically, in films you will be paid either by the day (as a "day player") or by the week; in television you can be paid by the day or week, or for a three-day half-week. New SAG and AFTRA contracts give the actor—for film or TV—a minimum of $414 per day (in 1989–90), and $1,440 for a week. In 1990-91 these figures go up to $431 a day and $1,498 a week, and in 1991-92 to $448 and $1,558. A three-day contract—which is for TV only—will net you $1,049 in 1989-90, $1,091 in 1990-91, and $1,135 in 1991-92. Increments apply for recurring roles and parts in longer shows.

These are just scale figures, however. Obviously you (or your agent) can try to negotiate more. What are your negotiating tools? They are not the same as those qualities that got you the job in the first place. Your actual salary will be determined mainly by your reputation and by the producers' need to have you. An industry is an industry, and nobody is going to spend $1,000 for you when someone just as good (or almost as good, unfortunately) can be had for $398.

Beginners in TV start out at scale plus 10% (with the 10% going to the agent); if you are a featured performer in a television show (more than a couple of lines), you will probably get a little more.

Established performers, whose names are known in the industry if not to the public at large, will get wages well over scale; perhaps $600 to $1,000 for a day's work in television, or $1,500-$2,500 per week on a half-hour show. Ordinarily there is a "top" salary for a TV show (one successful sitcom tops at $1,750, for example), but the occasional star can negotiate for "double-top" or even more, depending on a variety of circumstances. There's a great dividend for TV work, of course, as residual payments can double an actor's initial pay—and may often double it again (and again) if the series goes into syndication. The first rerun of an episode earns each of its actors another 100% of their original salaries, and subsequent (worldwide!) reruns can often provide sitcom performers with a small retirement income. But not all shows are rerun. On average, TV actors earn an additional 43% of their initial salary via subsequent rerun residuals.[42]

Moving Up

As you develop a growing reputation in the business, your salary may rise considerably. Daily salaries from $500 to $1,500 are certainly negotiable for filmwork, and on stage, $500-$750 per week is becoming common for strong career actors on the LORT circuit (sometimes LORT actors can also increase their stipends further by teaching in the theatre's attached conservatory). A well-respected veteran actor on Broadway may earn $2,000 per week without being a household celebrity.

These figures are "rule of thumb," but you should realize that a free-lance actor *with a good, solid reputation in the trade* can work *quite regularly* and still not make more than $20,000 a year in direct salary payments on television (twelve guest spots), films (four weeks' work on each of two films), or live theatre (four eight-week runs at $600). To be sure, $20,000 a year is a living wage, but you will have to be very lucky and very good to get it—and next year, of course, you might make only half that. Or less. Unlike other kinds of employment, acting is not steady or regular, which is to say you are never hired except for a brief period, usually measured in weeks, sometimes in days. You are *always* looking for work, and it doesn't necessarily get easier as you get better.

> PLAYBOY: You mean getting work is still a worry for you?
>
> HENRY FONDA: It's the operative problem. . . . You have no idea what your next job is, [so] you think, Well, that's it! I won't work again![43]

Bigger money, and even steady money, comes to the performer who lands a regular run in a television series; this occasionally happens to relatively inexperienced new performers. Even though an unknown performer can start out on a series making as little (relatively) as $1,500 per week, the regularity of the work multiplies this into a handsome sum. A person contracted to a series is guaranteed at least seven segments and generally will work at least thirteen. Regular salaries of $2,500 to $4,000 per segment can be paid to virtual newcomers if they are cast as leading series performers, and this mounts quickly if the show becomes a hit: $50,000 per episode is a fair fee for a series star in a hit show in its second or third year, and the actor's reputation will take it farther still.

Reputations, of course, multiply a TV and film actor's paycheck exponentially. No one in the business is unaware that "Cosby Show" star Bill Cosby earned about $100 million in 1987 (that was about five times more than Lee Iacocca), mostly from his TV show and its various spin-offs (including books). Michael J. Fox earned about $9 million that year, Paul Hogan $10 million, Arnold Schwarzenegger $18 million, and Sylvester Stallone (in a year without a *Rocky*) $21 million.

With name stars like these, of course, there are simply *no* rules of thumb. A name star is someone whose name alone will bring people to the box office, or bring the Neilson families to their television sets, or make people drink Coca-Cola rather than Pepsi. A star whose name is the major drawing card for a Broadway play can command a substantial fee for his or her box office appeal; Ed Asner and Madeleine Kahn, for example, were each reported to have received $20 thousand a week for headlining the 1989 Broadway revival of *Born Yesterday*. And a name star is considered "bankable," in the industry jargon of Hollywood, because a bank will finance a picture simply on the basis of the star's agreement to perform in it. The going rate for a bankable film star (such as Dustin Hoffman) now begins at $5 million per film, plus a share of the toy and tee-shirt subsidiaries. And, as mentioned at the beginning of this book, *Rocky V* will bring down $25 million to the Rock himself—this is a sum that would probably run your university's Theatre Department for the next seventy-five years.

The income potentially available from *commercials* is, of course, very high. But is this acting? Who knows, but if it doesn't ring the bells, it pays the bills. The performer in a TV commercial is paid a scale wage of $366.60 per shooting day, but then can receive literally thousands of dollars in residual income as the commercial is flashed across the tube ten times a day for six months. It is not true that the actor collects a residual income for each showing of a commercial (the contracts are extremely complex in figuring the actual payment), but the commercial that gets on the air will eventually bring its performers, on average, an additional four times the initial fee.[44] A few nationally distributed and long running spots can net the actor $10,000 or $20,000 or more, and some people—children, housewives, character types— can make up to a million dollars a year from this source. A few years ago a 9-year-old girl with no experience walked into an agent's office, was sent on an interview right away, and was hired on the spot to do a toothpaste advertisement. In a single day of toothy grins, nine different commercials were made, and a few years later she was richer by $27,000 for the day's experience. A more mature actor tells of having left the regional theatre, where he had been professionally active for more than six years, and going to Los Angeles to make films. Shortly after he arrived, he spent a day making several Di-Gel commercials. He eventually received $37,000 for the work—more that his total salary during the six years with LORT.

Still, the working actor must generally be considered in terms of poverty, not riches. There are over a hundred thousand professional actors today, and perhaps close to half a million with professional pretensions—and not 10,000 of them will really make a living at acting this year, and not 3,000 of them will make a living at it for the next five years in a row. Most hang in there for a while—a job here, a job there, a supplement here and there—and many hang on for the longest of long runs. Of these, only a very few will actually make enough income over a decade or so to raise a family or go out to Lutece or Chasen's for dinner instead of to the corner deli or the Taco Bell. That may not mean anything to you now, but will you still enjoy your tacos when you're 45? The question deserves at least a little of your time and consideration—right now.

CHAPTER 6

OTHER OPPORTUNITIES

If you've come this far, where are you?

You have talent, personality, contacts, training, a home base, a photo-resume, an agent, an interview technique, some knockout auditions, a union card, and now a first paying job.

You are at the beginning of your career. You know where to find out what you need from here on.

But a career is not merely begun, it must be sustained. That will require your constant attention, your every effort. Nothing comes easy to an actor, and nothing *stays* easy. The steps of the ladder are irregular; there are long gaps in between. And maybe when you get halfway up, you find the ladder isn't going where you wanted to go.

In this final section, take a look at some possibilities for acting professionally *outside* the established entertainment industries.

OUTSIDE THE INDUSTRY

Everything in this book, so far, is about how actors accommodate themselves to the existing theatre, film, and television industries— which, of course, have their own rules and procedures, and some of which may not thrill you as you get closer to them. "You've got to really be *sick* to want to be an actor here," says a well-known Hollywood agent. To be an industry actor means to stand, sit, smile, and squat on command, and often the command comes down from a source that you are hard pressed to respect.

Industry acting means schlepping about at your own expense, from office to office, from casting director to casting director, and being emotionally and financially subject to a ruling elite in which you may have no personal interest or sympathy.

Industry acting means spending most of your life looking for work, even when you are well into middle age. And most of your professional concentration won't be on developing the work itself, but rather on developing your network of contacts, and figuring out where the next job is coming from. That's exciting, to be sure, but will it be so in the coming years and decades? And how will you feel at 40 years old, being asked "So, tell me about yourself, Charley" by a casting director half your age? How will you feel at 60?

When you must audition and interview regularly for work, when that work is rarely won—and is transitory when (and if) it comes—you may begin to develop psychological problems. After all, it is *you* that you are putting up there on the stage, and it is you getting knocked down over and over. When rejection is piled atop rejection, no matter how many successes come in between, something happens in the pit of your stomach. Insecurity nibbles at your psyche, anxiety saps your nerve. Every job you lose must mean a personal flaw. You may retreat into a shell and self-destruct, or you may stuff yourself with bluster, and become a parody of your former self. Actors who defensively overinflate their egos, promoting their talents and sounding their trumpets upon the least occasions, become the most pathetic sights in New York and Hollywood. As the fine actor and director Austin Pendleton points out:

> Nothing bothers casting people more than the neurotic over-sell, and that is because an actor who oversells himself is an actor who does not trust himself and nothing, *nothing* disturbs show business professionals more than that. Self-mistrust is, after all, the ultimate buried nightmare for anybody in the business, as it is for bullfighters and tightrope-walkers.[45]

Are you a bullfighter or a tightrope-walker? Most actors fight contrary desires warring within them: a desire for security versus a lust for fame; a desire for personal happiness versus a need for artistic and emotional freedom. Many industry actors, even successful ones, find themselves virtual slaves to their profession, and are unable to make a personal decision without first consulting their agents, their producers, and their managers. Others enslave themselves to a set of industry conventions that are brutally dehumanizing. The vast majority are poor almost to the point of starvation. You can see why your parents paled when you told them you wanted to be an actor.

More and more people today are seeking, and finding, acting careers outside of the acting industries. These careers must be called compromising for those who seek solely to act for a living—they ordinarily require additional tasks and tangential skills—and they don't ordinarily offer even the distant hope for superstardom or super-wealth. If you are utterly committed to being a professional actor, you will probably find these quasi-acting careers unacceptable, and, for the truly committed actor, they probably *are* unacceptable. But you should take the opportunity to think about them, and about yourself as well, before heading off into the industry.

COMEDY

Stand-up comedy was one of the growth industries of the 1980s; at the beginning of that decade there were only a handful of professional comics, mainly filling spots on the Johnny Carson show and working the occasional Las Vegas or New York nightclub—and by the decade's end there were more than 2,000 pros working in 370 full time comedy clubs around the country, and on five network talk shows and forty weekly network/cable TV stand-up comedy programs. It was a virtual revolution: "The last time people saw this explosion of comedy was in the Depression, when vaudeville reached its height," says C. W. Metcalf, who runs a "corporate humor workshop."[46]

Some of these comics will almost certainly go on to become actors: as Steve Martin, Bill Cosby, and Roseanne Barr have done. Others—such as Johnny Carson—will probably star on (and produce) talk shows, and still others—like Jay Leno (Doritos tortilla chips) and Judy Tenuta (Diet Dr. Pepper)—will surely become comic spokespersons in TV commercials. And the other 1,995 will be making fees of $10 to $5,000 (or more) doing club comedy routines, opening nightclub acts, teaching "humor workshops" for business executives and some would-be comics, and performing corporate comedy warm-ups for various industrial sales conventions and in employee training films. Instructor/comics now staff a chain of thirty driving-safety schools sponsored by the California Department of Motor Vehicles.

Comedy can be a good way to make a living and develop your stage presence (and performance-media contacts) at the same time. Of course, you will need an inventive wit, an original style, a uniquely perceptive view of the world around you, and enormous quantities of self-motivation and ambition. If you have these goods, and that's a big "if," put together a knock-out act: comedy is a relatively easy field to break into, and you don't need scenery, a partner, or a role to audition for. Most clubs find time to look at new talent occasionally (some have an "amateur night" or an "open mike" night), and you can at least get seen without too much ado. Getting seen by Johnny or his talent scouts, however, requires more exposure than a single shot at your local club, so you will have to build up a repertoire of routines, and a repertoire of clubs you perform in, in order to move up the ladder.

ACADEMIC THEATRE

A second alternative is academic theatre. America doesn't yet have a national theatre, but we do have a series of publicly supported theatre and film-producing units in the nation's colleges and universities. These theatre, drama, video, and film departments, which began as academic branches of English, speech, and communications before (and shortly after) World War II, have become producing organizations that, within their obvious limitations, advance live theatre, and film and video art, in exciting ways. Hundreds of professional theatre artists now associate themselves, both part-time and full-time, with academic drama and film programs, partly for the financial security and prestige such positions can bring, and partly to have the freedom to work without commercial limitations.

A position with a university drama or film department will generally require you to *teach* acting—and/or directing, playwriting, filmmaking, dramatic literature, or theatre technique, usually for a nine-month academic year. This can leave you free to act professionally at summer theatres, and some institutions may offer some of the contacts to help bring this about. You may also be in a position to direct plays with students, and perhaps to act in student productions as well. Depending on the institution, you may have a high degree of freedom to teach and direct material you choose, and in a manner you choose. Academic employment in this form provides a reasonable annual salary and, at most institutions, a position with eventual job security (tenure) if you make the grade. Professors at the top of their profession can earn sizable salaries (over $75,000 for a nine-month academic year at some places) and move in some interesting circles, including professional theatres.

Academic life also provides an intellectual fervor, a great measure of artistic freedom, the excitement of working with young people, and, at some institutions, occasional sabbatical leaves (in addition to summers off) with full pay. Some institutions also run professional theatres, with faculty artists hired as the situation provides, thus giving you a chance to enjoy the best of both worlds.

But university theatres and film schools are academic, not professional, arts institutions, and any academic position entails a compromise of the highest professional standard. If you find daunting Shaw's famous phrase "If you can, do; if you can't teach," know that it will echo in your mind throughout your teaching career.

An academic position, as you would expect, requires far more in the way of intellectual and pedagogical preparation than does the ordinary Broadway or Hollywood or LORT career. University jobs are *not* easy to come by, nor are they easy to sustain. Many universities demand that their drama faculties publish books or articles in their areas of specialty (the well-known "publish or perish" formula), and all serious academic theatre departments require their staff members to develop and maintain active careers, either as scholars (evidenced by publication), or as professional-level actors, directors, or theatre artists (evidenced by successful artistic works both on and off the campus). The best institutions also demand excellent teaching, as evidenced by sound and innovative pedagogies (teaching plans and theories), students that look good on stage and get work when they graduate, and good teaching evaluations. A successful academic career, therefore, is every bit as professional and as demanding as the acting careers we have heretofore been discussing.

If you are interested in pursuing a career in academic theatre, you should *at minimum* earn an M.F.A degree from a highly reputable institution—the best that you can get into. If possible, seek a Ph.D. as well. Choose a field of interest and read everything you can about it; develop some new ideas of your own. Learn one or two foreign languages, particularly as they may be useful in your field of interest. Attend scholarly conventions (the Association for Theatre in Higher Education—ATHE—is the umbrella organization in this area), and find out how you can make an artistic or intellectual contribution to future conventions. You will make your strongest job application by developing a professional reputation along with your academic one. Write and publish some scholarly essays or play reviews, or establish yourself as a director or actor with a summer theatre, LORT theatre, off-Broadway theatre, or other professional group. Write plays, or translate them, and get them produced. Make a name for yourself *somewhere*, for there are literally hundreds of applications for every drama faculty opening, even at institutions of modest repute, and your application needs the cachet of something special besides your academic degree and your splendid faculty recommendations.

The job market for drama faculty aspirants is year-round, but most positions begin in September, with the application period beginning the previous fall. Openings are widely advertised by law (how refreshing, for readers of this book), and you should check the monthly listings in *Joblist*, published by ATHE (P.O. Box 15282, Evansville, Indiana 47716; you must join the organization first to get a copy), and the twice-monthly *Artsearch*, put out by TCG (355 Lexington Avenue, New York, NY 10017). If your training and interests are more on the literary side, you should also check the positions listed by the Modern Language Association (MLA). ATHE holds a national convention every summer, where you'll find a number of last-minute academic posts available to ATHE-registered jobseekers.

Successful university drama and film instructors are invariably people who have a love for teaching, for academic freedom, and for the university life. Teaching, on the other hand, may be a very unhappy alternative for the person captivated by the wish to act professionally, or who is intellectually insecure. A university instructor is simply not a professional actor or director, but a professional educator, and would-be actors who go on to graduate school only to get a degree "to fall back on" may never find much satisfaction on a college campus. Essentially, an academic program is still one of scrutiny and analysis as much as it is of production and performance. Academic life is fascinating to anyone driven by curiosity and a desire for knowledge; but it is a supreme bore for someone looking only for the thrill of the follow-spot or the film studio. And, as it involves as much effort to become a successful professor as a successful actor, it cannot be recommended that a budding actor expect to "fall back" on the profession of teaching. You will probably only fall back on your back.

YOUR OWN COMPANY

For the performer who wants to create and perform, but has little or no interest in academia, there is a third alternative between the industries and the campus, and that is the private, nonunion theatre company. Some of the most exciting and artistic work in America and abroad has, in the past, been done by such "amateur" companies, under the leadership of such near legendary figures as Konstantin Stanislavski, André

Antoine, Jacques Copeau, and Jerzy Grotowski; and such moderns as Ronnie Davis, Robert Wilson, Paul Sills, Joseph Chaikin, Charles Ludlam, Julian Beck, and Andre Gregory. Such work is going on today as well; you may already know of a theatre collective or experimental group in or near your own town.

Such works often flower into full-blown professional operations, if that's what their directors wish. David Emmes and Martin Benson, together with several fellow graduates of San Francisco State University, created a tiny amateur theatre in an abandoned dockside warehouse in 1964—in 1988, the South Coast Repertory Theatre won the Tony Award for best regional theatre, and many of the original members, along with Emmes and Benson, work there still. Three University of California students—among those to whom the first edition of this book was dedicated—created the Lexington Conservatory Theatre at an unused barn in upstate New York in 1973; that company became the Capital Repertory LORT Theatre of Albany in 1980. Two others from the same group created the Ukiah Playhouse in northern California, which, while still nonunion, is paying its staff, touring the Northwest, and building its own theatre building.

Amateur theatres begin and operate outside the established unions or industry. Some such groups may have a short life, to be sure, but some develop an enviable measure of security. Many are communal in both art and living arrangements. Most of these groups try to make ends meet at the box office, some survive with local or foundation grants, and some thrive for a generation or more without ever going under union auspices. Some—let's go all the way here—tour the world and create theatrical history: That's certainly true of Julian and Malina Beck's Living Theatre, Ronnie Davis's San Francisco Mime Troupe, and the Chicago Steppenwolf Company.

There's nothing to prevent you from looking up and joining one of these groups, if they will take you, and there's nothing to prevent you from starting up your own. All it takes is a building, some friends, some paint and plywood, and some energy and ideas. And ideals. True, you will have to work in the daytime at "regular" jobs in order to be free to rehearse at night, but if you are doing what makes you happy, you will be well rewarded. For most people, the urge to perform need not be satisfied by working on Broadway, in Hollywood, or on the Yale Drama School stage; it could be quite satisfactorily fulfilled by acting with friends before a small audience in your own home town. You should certainly consider this option before you pack your bags for either coast. Some of the most genuinely artistic work in the country is done at theatres like these.

As is true with the theatre, so it is true with film. The rapid growth of independent filmmaking in America in recent decades has been extraordinary, and a large group of nonunion amateur filmmakers is growing up nationwide. They have a literature, a character, and an opportunity to exchange presentations. Student and amateur films are being commercially marketed, too, so that a venture into independent filmmaking does not necessarily cut off all professional possibilities.

Television is entering a new age of decentralization that, at this point, holds even greater promise of diversified development. Camcorders and videocassettes, as well as the commercial availability of home recording systems and studios, augur an international flow of televised production that may or may not be professional in character. Video art is a recognized new form of expression that has been shown increasingly in museums and galleries during the past decade, and is developing commercial possibilities, even for actors. Local and national cable programming is now a new market for video art and videodrama, and dozens of companies are now entering the field of satellite distribution of original and rebroadcast television programming. "Superstations" now broadcast nationally and internationally, and airwave deregulation has permitted various experiments in specialized telecasting.

What does this all mean? Overall, it means less network and mass-medium television production; and more local, specialized, and innovative production, providing new potential for close-to-home training, employment, and creative artistry in the video-acting arts. So the Hollywood connection is not your only track to a professional career in video performance. Your camcorder and a few friends might provide a start.

OTHER THEATRE JOBS

Finally, you should be aware of the tremendous number of jobs in the theatre that are less visible than acting, but more widely available. Some of them you are probably quite familiar with: director, designer, technician, playwright, and stage manager. Others are described in the previous pages: agent, casting director, producer, production assistant, publicist. Chances are you haven't studied these professions—no courses exist for them in most colleges and universities—but they are, in fact, significant career options for thousands of persons trained in drama.   There are far more jobs in these areas than for actors, and far fewer people clamoring to break in.   There are even areas where the demand for talent exceeds the supply.

Such employment, of course, can lead to professional acting further on, if you're still game to get on stage. It may also lead to things you find you like even better than acting. Even very successful actors—Richard Benjamin and Ron Howard are good examples—found a career change into directing inestimably rewarding at a certain point. Writing, casting, and producing are also where a number of ex-actors wind up, and they're usually very happy to be there. Some actors happily sit out the "middle years" of their adult lives in such positions, and then return to acting in their senior years. Casting director Burt Remsen, acting teacher Lee Strasberg, and director/educator John Houseman enjoyed stunning success as actors long after establishing themselves as masters in other mid-life career positions. Acting is one of only two professions in which you can start out—and rise to the top—wholly during your later life (being president of the United States is the other, as an ex-actor proved).

APPENDIX

I have resisted the temptation to provide a list of agent and casting director addresses below, although they're very easy to come by. It takes about a year for any book to come out, from the time of its drafting to its appearance on the bookshelf, and in that year 10% of the phone numbers I would list here would already be out of date. There's no business as volatile, as rapid in turnover as show business. Is there another business whose standard directory is revised *monthly* (the *Ross Reports*, which flags more than 100 address or personnel changes each issue)? And no business is as susceptible to the ups and downs of hits, flops, blockbusters, and turkeys that change the status of its participants overnight.

Besides, freshly updated lists of addresses are readily available, for free or for nominal amounts, when you will actually need them. And they can be obtained in convenient packages, such as in preaddressed mailing labels, or in geographically coordinated "mapped-out" listings.

Therefore, the appendix to this book is an attempt to list some reasonably permanent *sources* of up-to-the-minute information that you can tap with a single visit or phone call.

I've also, for the most part, left out exact prices. The costs of services mentioned in this book have tripled or quadrupled since the first edition, and will no doubt continue to rise as rapidly. Indeed, the price of *this* book has more than tripled. Inflation has hit the labor-intensive acting industries as hard or harder than it has the country at large, and the theatrical capitals, New York and southern California, are inflation leaders, as anyone who has tried to stay in a hotel recently in either town well knows. But the prices for the materials listed here are all reasonable; all the listings books, for example, should cost about the same as a movie ticket or two at the time you read this. The general trade books (which are bigger and more expensive) will cost about what similar books cost in other fields; so you may want to read them in a school or public library.

WHERE TO GO FOR PUBLISHED INFORMATION

In New York you can find virtually any material published about acting, including trade papers, journals, and books, at either of two great shops: the Drama Book Shop, 723 Seventh Avenue, NY 10019 (call them at [212] 944-0595), and Applause Books, 211 West 71st St, NY 10023 ([212] 787-8858). You should certainly head to one or both of these delightfully welcoming havens immediately upon arrival in New York. The personable employees of each are theatre buffs themselves—often actors as well—and can offer you advice on the latest updated listings (and other) books. You'll also see flyers of what's going on in town, and even notices of rooms for rent. Trade papers are also sold regularly at newsstands in the Times Square area, and elsewhere in midtown Manhattan.

If you're out of town and want the latest books, trade papers, or updated listings, you can call either of these shops and order by phone, using a credit card, subject to a minimum charge ($25 at time of writing).

In Los Angeles, the Samuel French Theatre Bookshop, 7623 Sunset Boulevard (off Stanley) has everything you can imagine; it's an outstanding drama and film bookstore, in addition to being the West Coast outlet for the French library of plays. You can call them too, at [213] 876-0570.

You can pick up trade papers around any of the motion picture studios, or at the outdoor Universal News Agency stand at 1655 Las Palmas (just off Hollywood Boulevard) which carries many actor-oriented periodicals—some available nowhere else in town. The Las Palmas stand also has your hometown newspaper, if you're getting homesick (or want to check on what's happening at the Seattle Rep). Also of interest, particularly for older theatre and film books, is Larry Edmunds' Cinema and Theatre Book Shop, around the corner at 6658 Hollywood Boulevard.

Maybe you want to sit in a comfortable library and read from a great collection of acting books, plus up-to-date journals in the field. If so, there are two wonderful places for you. In New York, it's the Library of the Performing Arts in Lincoln Center (upstairs is the magnificent Theatre Collection of the New York Public Library, which has clippings from America's earliest theatre days). In Los Angeles, it's the Margaret Herrick Library at the Academy of Motion Picture Arts and Sciences (8949 Wilshire Boulevard, Beverly Hills, 4th floor). Both are free. The Library of the Performing Arts is open daily except Sunday, and the Herrick Library is open Monday, Tuesday, Thursday, and Friday. The Herrick Library emphasizes the literature of film (this is the academy of the Academy Awards), but there are plenty of materials on all the other media as well.

TRADE PAPERS

In Los Angeles:

Hollywood Reporter (largely film/TV), daily

Variety (largely film/TV), daily

Drama-Logue (largely stage), weekly

In New York:

Back Stage (comprehensive, casting section insert), weekly

Show Business (largely stage), weekly

Variety (comprehensive), weekly

LISTINGS BOOKS

Whatever else, actors need a bunch of addresses and phone numbers in order to get around. Actually, just about everything you will need is in the telephone book, but that's a bit hefty to carry about on interviews. The following listings books are a bit handier, and include some harder-to-find (and unlisted) numbers and extensions; also, they are updated more often than the phone book, which in this business is important. The books are available at the shops above (you can order them by phone in most cases), or you can write directly to the publisher. All are reasonably priced, but since most are updated regularly, the exact price at the time you will want them cannot be accurately predicted here.

(*Also note*: There is a very high turnover in this field of quasi-literary endeavor; many of the listings books noted in the last *Acting Professionally* edition no longer exist, and many of those listed here may not be in the shops by the time you are. But there will be others, you can be sure.)

New York and Hollywood Listings

The Agencies. Published by Acting World Books, P. O. Box 3044, Hollywood, CA 90078. An *annotated* listing of West Coast theatrical agencies, with addresses and phones, updated monthly. Identifies major agents in each firm, describes major fields covered (motion pictures, TV, live stage (Equity), commercials, children, voice-over, literary, and so on), often indicates agencies looking for new talent, identifies phonies and frauds, usually gives brief evaluation of agency's reputation. As reliable as this sort of publication can be (they try!).

Note: Acting World Books also publishes a series of useful booklets on the acting trade; they call them "seminars to go," on subjects such as "how to get, work with, and keep the best agent for you."

CD (Casting Directors) *Directory.* Published by Breakdown Services, Ltd. 8242 W. Third Street, #250, Los Angeles, CA 90048. A comprehensive and regularly updated listing of Los Angeles casting directors. Published quarterly.

Note: Breakdown Services also publishes lists of agents, casting directors, and producers on mailing labels, for direct mailings of photo-resumes, postcards, and so on.

Extra Casting Agencies & More, independently published at P. O. Box 3102, Glendale, CA 91201 (818) 953-4078. The Spring 1989 issue lists 50 extra casting agencies in Los Angeles, plus ten in New York, seven in Chicago, and others in Denver, Miami, Santa Fe, Toronto, and Vancouver.

Henderson's Mailing Labels. Same business; mailing labels of casting directors, agents, and so on; available in New York.

The Hollywood Acting Coaches and Teachers Directory. Just what it says, and annotated, too. Published by Acting World Books (see above), and updated regularly.

Hollywood Reporter Studio Blu Book, 6715 Sunset Boulevard, Los Angeles, CA 90028. A complete annual listing of talent agents, producers, and advertising agencies.

L.A.'s & N.Y.'s Casting Directors. Written by Wendy Shawn. Published twice a year by Castbusters, P.O. Box 67C75, Los Angeles, CA

90067. Fully annotated, with lengthy descriptions of close to 100 casting offices in L.A., and another 36 in N.Y.

Ross Reports Television. Published by Television Index, Inc., 150 Fifth Avenue, New York, NY 10011. Outstanding, and very official. Revised *monthly*; lists personnel and policies on seeing actors for New York agents, New York casting directors, New York TV studios and offices, West Coast production studios, and Los Angeles casting personnel.

SD (Pacific Coast Studio Directory), 6313 Yucca Street, Hollywood, CA 90028-5093. Comprehensive listings of West Coast production companies, casting directors, television stations, union offices, helicopter pilots, trained animals, and just about everything else in show biz, *except* actor agents. Published quarterly.

Listings of Summer Theatres, Regional Theatres, Dinner Theatres, and Outdoor Theatres

The best shall come first:

Jill Charles, *Regional Theatre Directory*

Jill Charles, *Summer Theatre Directory*

Both Ms. Charles's books are published by Dorset Theatre Festival and Colony House, Inc., and are available from theatre bookshops or from Theatre Directories, P.O. Box 519, Dorset, VT 05251. The listings are comprehensive and authoritative, and are annotated with useful information, such as salaries paid, number of non-Equity positions available, audition tips, and others. Ms. Charles is a theatre producer, and well understands what actors need to know.

You may also look at John Allen's books, which, though a bit breezier, are also very informative.

John Allen, *The Summer Theatre Guide: From an Actor's Viewpoint.*

John Allen, *The Regional & Dinner Theatre Guide: From an Actor's Viewpoint.*

Both are published by Allen Theatrical Publications, P.O. Box 2129, New York, NY 10185.

You will also find useful:

Theatre Directory, published by Theatre Communications Group (TCG), 355 Lexington Avenue, New York, NY 10017. This pamphlet lists nearly 250 nonprofit professional theatre and related service organizations, and is updated each year. Inexpensive.

Theatre Profiles, also published by TCG, usually every two years. The same as above, but with photos, descriptions, past production schedules, financial information, and so on.

Summer Theatre, published in early spring each year by Show Business, Inc., 1501 Broadway, #2900, New York, NY 10036 (telephone: [212] 354-7607). And the same company's trade paper, *Show Business*, routinely prints updated lists of dinner theatre, LORT theatres, and industrial producers, as well as casting directors, personal managers, New York producers, and others. Not all this information appears in every issue, but it does appear regularly.

The Institute of Outdoor Drama, CB# 3240, Graham Memorial, University of North Carolina, Chapel Hill, NC 27599-3240, provides an annual listing of nearly 60 outdoor dramas, together with relevant information on schedules, salaries, and personnel. The listing, which comes out in late February, is free. The institute also holds unified auditions in Chapel Hill for 15 of these productions each March; write for further information well ahead of time. Send them a self-addressed, stamped envelope for reply.

On request, Actors' Equity Association will send you a list of "theatres where the Membership Candidate Program may be in effect." Emphasis is on "*may* be"—even Equity is not always sure. Close to 250 LORT, SPT, LOA, stock, and dinner theatres are listed, with addresses. Free, but pick it up in person, or send them a stamped, self-addressed envelope.

Apprenticeship programs are offered by numerous professional and university theatres. The University/Resident Theatre Association (U/RTA), 1540 Broadway, Suite 704, New York, NY 10036 is a good source of information, as are summer theatre publications. Or write directly to professional theatre companies for information.

BOOKS WHERE YOU LIST

These are the books where you place your photo. If you qualify to get in, *do it*; these books are the bibles of casting offices, and if you catch a casting director in a spare moment, chances are he/she is thumbing through these pages, looking for just the right person. You don't buy these books; you just buy into them.

> *Players Directory* (officially *Academy Players Directory*; this is from the folks that issue the Oscars and operate the Herrick Library), 8949 Wilshire Boulevard, Beverly Hills, CA 90211. Accepts photo submissions from SAG members, or from *signed* clients of SAG-franchised agencies. Published three times a year. You must classify yourself as a leading woman, leading man, ingenue, younger leading man, male or female character/comedian(ienne), child male, or child female. You can also list your ethnicity and handicap.

> *Players Guide*, 165 West 46th Street, New York, NY 10036. Published annually, it covers stage actors, as well as actors in film and TV. Accepts submissions only from members of Equity, SAG, or AFTRA.

BOOKS ABOUT ACTING AND ACTORS

This is a select list of books you might wish to have in your personal collection, or read in a theatre library.

Arlen, Michael J. *Thirty Seconds.* New York: Farrar, Strauss & Giroux, 1980. An amusing and insightful look into the making of a television commercial.

Barr, Tony. *Acting for the Camera.* Boston: Allyn & Bacon, 1981. The best book available on film and television acting by a veteran actor, producer, and teacher.

Bayer, William. *Breaking Through, Selling Out, Dropping Dead, and Other Notes on Filmmaking.* New York: Delta Books, 1973. A stunning analysis of Hollywood from a unique point of view.

Callan, K. *The L.A. Agent Book.* Studio City, CA: Sweden Press, 1988. Outstanding survey of agents, plus a great many "inside tips."

Callan, K. *The N.Y. Agent Book.* Same publisher, same theme, different city, 1987.

Callan, K. *How to Sell Yourself as an Actor.* Same publisher, 1988. The third in a very helpful series.

Cohen, Robert. *Acting Power.* Mountain View, CA: Mayfield, 1978; and

Acting One, same publisher, 1984. An approach to acting, and an introductory text on the same theme, by the author of the current book.

Haskins, Dennis. *Rating the Agents.* Vol. II. No publisher listed, 1988. This is a fascinating tabulation of the actual jobs received by various L.A. agents for their clients in fall 1987. It is only marginally scientific, but the general results are revealing if unsurprising (the biggest agencies generally score the most jobs, but there are some interesting exceptions).

Henry, Mari Lyn, and Rogers, Lynne. *How to Be a Working Actor.* New York: M. Evans and Company, 1986. A book not unlike this one, with lots of good information. Ms. Henry is a casting director, Ms. Rogers an actress, and their writing is lively and informed.

Fridell, Squire. *Acting in Television Commercials.* New York: Harmony Books, 1980. Best in the field. Informative and cleverly illustrated.

Gam, Rita. *Actors: A Celebration.* New York: St. Martin's Press, 1988. Breezy interviews and discussions of male superstars (Jack Lemmon, Charlton Heston), classical stage actors (Derek Jacobi, Len Cariou, Ben Kingsley), and "the new breed of star" (Jeremy Irons, Treat Williams), by an important actress in her own right.

Gam, Rita. *Actress to Actress.* New York: Nick Lyons Books, 1986. Same theme, with ladies: Jane Fonda, Meryl Streep, Grace Kelly, Zoe Caldwell, Joanne Woodward, many others.

Goldman, William. *The Season: A Candid Look At Broadway.* New York: Harcourt Brace Jovanovich, 1969. A candid and acid look at the Broadway theatre; still pertinent.

Hagen, Uta. *Respect for Acting.* New York: MacMillan, 1973. A gentle and instructive book on acting written by a fine actress and teacher; particularly interesting because it shows the way a New York actor thinks as well as acts.

Jessup, Cortland, with Alpert, S. Lee. *The Actor's Guide to Breaking into TV Commercials.* New York: Pilot Books, 1980.

Lakein, Alan. *How to Get Control of Your Time and Your Life.* New York: David McKay, 1973. One young New York actor describes this as an *absolute* must. It may help you achieve a *professional* attitude.

Shacter, Susan. *Caught in the Act: New York Actors Face to Face.* New York: NAL Books, 1986. Interviews with Christopher Reeve, Kevin Kline, John Lithgow, Edward Herrmann, Tom Hulce, William Hurt, John Malkovich, Raul Julia, Harvey Fierstein, and forty-five others, all men.

Shurtleff, Michael. *Audition*. New York: Walker and Co., 1978.
    An outstanding book, not only for its advice on auditioning, but for its
    general information about the acting process.

You should be aware that there are a number of "junk" books on
the market that purport to tell you how to break into the movies, leap
onto the stage, or turn into a star in three easy lessons. One (*How to Get
into the Movies* by Diane Morang) advises: "After interviewing with as
many agents as you can, make a decision as to with which agency you
would like to sign."

UNION OFFICES

Current lists of franchised agents are available at the following union
offices, but you must pick them up in person. There may be a nominal
charge.

In New York:

Actors' Equity Association, 165 West 46th Street, New York, NY
10019. Receptionist on second floor.

Screen Actors' Guild, 1700 Broadway, New York, NY 10019

American Federation of Television and Radio Artists, 1350
Avenue of the Americas, New York, NY 10019

In Los Angeles:

Actors' Equity Association, 4630 Sunset Boulevard, Los Angeles,
CA 90028

Screen Actors' Guild, 7065 Hollywood Boulevard, Hollywood,
CA 90028

American Federation of Television and Radio Artists, 6922
Hollywood Boulevard, Hollywood, CA 90028

SCHOOLS OF THEATRE AND ACTING

Colleges and universities offering major programs in drama are
numerous and located everywhere in the country. Some colleges are
principally graduate schools, and others are primarily undergraduate.
The best listings, with a good deal of basic information, are in Jill

Charles's *Directory of Theatre Training Programs*, P.O. Box 519, Dorset, VT 05251. You can also look up general information on America's 3,000 colleges and universities in *Peterson's Guide*, available in most libraries. You should also send for literature from the University/ Resident Theatre Association (U/RTA), 1540 Broadway, Suite 704, New York, NY 10036.

In addition, there are also pages of advertisements from many drama training programs in certain theatre journals: *American Theatre* (published by TCG) has the most, but *Theatre Journal*, *Performing Arts Journal*, and *The Drama Review* also have ads and occasionally articles on theatre education in America. These journals are in most university libraries and are sold at theatre bookshops. Back Stage also publishes a *College Guide to the Performing Arts* each November, as a subsection of their weekly trade magazine; this issue includes over one hundred school listings and ads.

There are noncollegiate schools, too, of course, mostly in New York and Los Angeles. Most advertise in the trades. The following are some currently well-known schools.

In New York:

The American Academy of Dramatic Arts, 120 Madison Avenue, NY 10016. Established 1884; offers a two-year course in daytime or evenings to high school graduates.

Herbert Berghof Studio, 120 Bank Street, NY 10014. Established by Berghof and his wife, Uta Hagen, in 1945; offers courses during four seasonal terms. You may sign up for as few or as many as you wish.

The Lee Strasberg Theatre Institute, 115 East 15th Street, NY 10003. Mr. Strasberg died in 1982, but his teachings continue.

The Juilliard School. An outstanding program allied with the famous music conservatory in Lincoln Center.

Neighborhood Playhouse, 340 East 54th Street, NY 10022. Founded and still run by the celebrated Sandy Meisner, the Playhouse offers a full-time program to high school graduates, during which time students "are not permitted to seek or accept engagements to appear in public, either on the amateur or professional stage."

Sonia Moore Studio of the Theatre, 251 West 80th Street. (Mailing address: 485 Park Avenue, NY 10022.) Devoted to the Stanislavski "system."

In Los Angeles:

(Phone numbers are a better contact point with L.A. schools.)

American Academy of Dramatic Arts/West, Pasadena— (818) 798-0777. A branch of the venerable institution.

Estelle Harmon Actors Workshop—(213) 931-8137. Long-time in the field.

Film Actors' Workshop—(818) 766-5108. Run by Tony Barr, author of the excellent *Acting for the Camera.*

The Lee Strasberg Theatre Institute—(213) 650-7777. A branch of the New York school. "You come on stage to be alive, not to act," they advertise.

All of these schools, of course, charge tuition and have facilities for study and work. Most present plays before invited audiences of producers and agents.

WHERE TO LIVE IN NEW YORK OR LOS ANGELES

It's expensive. There are, however, some youth hostels opening as this book goes to press; they're good for short, get-acquainted stays at rock bottom prices. In New York, the hostel is at 891 Amsterdam Ave. (at West 103rd Street); call (212) 431-7100 for information. In L.A. (Santa Monica, actually), it's at 1436 2nd St.; call (213) 831-8846. The L.A. hostel is in the Rapp saloon, a former movie studio, which is appropriate. Both offer accommodations in the $12 (L.A.) to $20 (N.Y.) range, in 1989 prices.

NOTES

1. William Shallert, in the *Los Angeles Times*, March 22, 1980.

2. *Los Angeles Times*, 28 December 1988.

3. "The film business . . . , " James Monaco, in Monaco, *American Film Now*. New York: Oxford, 1979, p. 47.

4. Francine Witkin, in *Drama-Logue*, July 24, 1980.

5. *Final Cut*. New York: Seabury Press, 1974, p. 47-8.

6. The Movie Business . . . ,William Bluem and Jason Squire, eds. New York: Hastings House, 1972.

7. "Almost always . . . , " Donald Farber, in Farber, *From Option to Opening*. New York: Drama Book Shop Publications, 1968, p. 99.

8. *Los Angeles Times*, 15 May 1987.

9. Pauline Kael, "Why Are the Movies So Bad?" *The New Yorker*, June 23, 1980, p. 88.

10. William Gillette, in *The Illusion of the First Time in Acting*. New York: Dramatic Museum of Columbia University, 1915, p. 45.

11. In Susan Shacter, *Caught in the Act*. New York: NAL, 1986, p. 45.

12. Bud Robinson, in *Drama-Logue*, August 28, 1980.

13. *Los Angeles Times*, 29 August 1982.

14. William Bayer, *Breaking Through, Selling Out, Dropping Dead, and Other Notes on Filmmaking*. New York: Delta Book, 1973. A stunning analysis of Hollywood from a unique point of view.

15. *Los Angeles Times*, 11 January 1989.

16. Documentation in "Women and Minorities in Television Drama, 1969-78," edited by George Gerbner and Nancy Signorielli, released by the University of Pennsylvania and the Screen Actors Guild, October 29, 1979.

17. Hermione Gingold, in William Fadiman, *Hollyood Now*. New York: Liveright, 1972, p. 82.

18. Bobby Hoffman, in *Drama-Logue*, July 3, 1980.

19. Suzanne Pleshette, in *Drama-Logue*, July 17, 1980.

20. Ruth Gordon, In *Drama-Logue*, July 3, 1980.

21. George Bernard Shaw, preface to *Man and Superman*.

22. Mark Lamos, in *Drama-Logue*, June 19, 1980.

23. Shelley Winters, in John Gruen, *Close-Up*. New York: Viking, 1968, p. 48ff.

24. Georgina Spelvin, in the *Los Angeles Times*, July 12, 1980.

25. Mike Fenton, in *Newsweek,* March 14, 1977.

26. Rene Auberjonois, in "The Regional Theatre, Four Views," *The Drama Review,* Fall, 1968.

27. In Susan Shacter, *Caught in the Act.* New York: St. Martin's Press, 1988, p. 75.

28. K. Callan, *The L.A. Agent Book.* Studio City, Calif.: Sweden Press, 1988, p. 7.

29 William Bayer, *Breaking Through , Selling Out, Dropping Dead, and Other Notes on Filmmaking.* New York: Delta Books, 1973.

30. Jerold Franks, in *Drama-Logue,* June 5, 1980.

31. Mike Hanks, in *Drama-Logue,* June 5, 1980.

32. Richard Dreyfuss, in Gordon Hunt, *How to Audition.* New York: Harper & Row, 1977), p. 303.

33. *Denver Post,* interview with Alan Carter, 19 June 1988.

34. Michael Shurtleff, in *Audition.* New York: Walder and Co., 1978.

35. *Drama-Logue,* 16 December 1982, quoted by Gary Ballard.

36. Hal Prince, in Gordon Hunt, *How to Audition.* New York: Harper & Row, 1977, p. 303.

37. "The most successful people . . . , " Chuck Blore, in *Commercials Monthly.* June 1980.

38. Cortland Jessup with S. Lee Alpert, in *The Actor's Guide to Breaking into TV Commercials.* New York: Pilot Books, 1980.

39. Beverly Sanders, in *Commercials Monthly,* June 1980.

40. Jason Robards, in Howard Greenberger, *The Off-Off Broadway Experience.* Englewood Cliffs, N.J.: Prentice-Hall, 1971.

41. This quotation compiled from interviews in the *New York Times,* 5 January 1989 and *Theatre Week,* 23-29 January, 1989.

42. In 1988, TV actors earned $309 million, of which about $216 million came in direct payments and about $93 million came as residuals.

43. *Playboy,* December 1981.

44. Of the $344.5 million earned by SAG actors in TV commercials in 1988, more that $275 million, or 80%, came through residual payments.

45. Austin Pendleton, in *Yale Theatre,* Fall 1973.

46. Figures and quotation from the *New York Times,* 9 April 1989 p. F17.